THE
FRENCH
REVOLUTION

A TALE OF TERROR AND HOPE
FOR OUR TIMES

T0385698

In Memory of Evelyn

THE
FRENCH
REVOLUTION

A TALE OF TERROR AND HOPE FOR OUR TIMES

HAROLD BEHR

sussex
ACADEMIC
PRESS
Brighton • Chicago • Toronto

2 4 6 8 10 9 7 5 3 1

First published in 2015 by
SUSSEX ACADEMIC PRESS
PO Box 139
Eastbourne BN24 9BP

and in the United States of America by
SUSSEX ACADEMIC PRESS
Independent Publishers Group
814 N. Franklin Street, Chicago, IL 60610

and in Canada by
SUSSEX ACADEMIC PRESS (CANADA)
24 Ranee Avenue, Toronto, Ontario M6A 1M6

British Library Cataloguing in Publication Data
A CIP catalogue record for this book is available from the British Library.

Library of Congress Cataloging-in-Publication Data
Behr, Harold.
The French Revolution : a tale of terror and hope for our times / Harold
  Behr.
pages cm
Includes bibliographical references and index.
ISBN 978-1-84519-703-2 (pb : alk. paper)
  1. France—History—Revolution, 1789–1799—Psychological aspects.
2. Revolutions—France—Psychological aspects. 3. Revolutionaries—
France—Psychology. I. Title.
DC158.8.B44 2015
944.04—dc23

2014037590

Typeset and designed by Sussex Academic Press, Brighton & Eastbourne.
Printed by TJ International, Padstow, Cornwall.
This book is printed on acid-free paper.

Contents

A Personal Note

It may help you to follow my train of thought, dear reader, if you know that I am one of those people who starts a journey without any clear sense of my route or even my destination until I get there. As soon as the words land on the page I begin to notice interesting scenery which attracts my attention and encourages me to stop by at places I hadn't thought to visit in the first place. However, in order to centre you I will preface my text with a chronology of the French Revolution which I hope will act as a point of reference to my subsequent meanderings.

The French Revolution has interested me since my schooldays. Brought up in *apartheid* South Africa, where talk of revolution was never far from the surface, I used to wonder what form a modern revolution would take in a country where injustice was so blatant and suffering so manifest. South Africa, it seemed, was a revolution waiting to happen. The fact that it didn't take place is probably due in large measure to the political genius and magnanimity of Nelson Mandela.

This led me to ponder the role of leadership at a time of social unrest. My question was (and still is): Are leaders created by the people out of a particular social need or do certain personalities with vision and purpose project themselves into positions of leadership by pointing the way forward and shaping the minds of the people on how best to meet their need? By the same token how does society rid itself of leaders who fail in their mission, especially when there are no democratic structures in place to ease the transition?

The French Revolution, a seething mix of social unrest, revolution and war, provides an ideal laboratory for investigating these questions and applying the findings to any of the numerous upheavals which have continued to shake the world from 1789 up to the present time. The first two decades of the twenty-first century are seeing an upsurge of violence driven by nationalistic and religious passions riding on the back of territorial claims. The focus has drifted away from Western Europe to Africa and the Middle East. As I write a conflagration is sputtering over Russia's territorial claims to Eastern Ukraine; Islamic fundamentalists are sweeping through Iraq, engaged in a jihadi war to convert or destroy Christian communities and the entrenched Israeli-

Palestinian conflict has lurched into a new downward spiral of implacable hostility and mutual allegations of criminal behaviour and genocidal intent.

At first sight the French Revolution seems like a storm in a teacup compared to twentieth- and twenty-first century violence perpetrated on a massive scale. But if we set aside the magnification of latter day violence conferred on us by technological advances in weaponry and communications we see the same justifications, the same emotions and the same patterns of group dynamics unfolding in 2014 as in 1789. Today we have a better understanding of the origins of violence but we still seem to be light years away doing anything about it.

As someone who delights in controversy but hates violence I was initially drawn to the life of Maximilien Robespierre, the idealist turned monster. A psychiatrist friend of mine, hoping no doubt to analyse me on the spot, demanded to know why I was interested in 'the bad man of the French Revolution'. I still don't know, but I have been intrigued to discover that more than two-and-a-half centuries later the ghost of this man continues to divide people into his fierce detractors (the many) and his starry-eyed admirers (the few).

Several biographies later I came to see Robespierre in his social context as a phenomenon of the Revolution which he helped to shape. Not only was he a phenomenon but a symbol. People who vote for the Revolution, and indeed people who vote for revolutions in general, also tend to cast their vote for Robespierre in conjunction with the principles he stood for. For others, he is the personification of the Reign of Terror. This leads me to another controversy: Was the Terror an inevitable part of the Revolution or was it an aberration from the otherwise smoothly flowing movement for the rights of the people?

I discovered many other controversies hidden in the woodwork, all revolving around questions of goodness and badness. Was Louis XVI, for instance, a well-intentioned guy doing his best in bad circumstances (Louis the Nice) or was he a weak, arrogant, contemptuous and contemptible pawn in the hands of his wife and her selfish cronies? (Louis the Nasty). And how important was his personality when it came to determining his own fate and the fate of France?

And then there was Danton. Was he a blustering, bloated double-dealing terrorist or was he a humane, diplomatic statesman caught in the wrong place at the wrong time? And Marat? Was he the filthy monster he is so often portrayed as or a deeply passionate defender of the poor and the dispossessed? And so on.

I decided that the only way to unmuddle myself was to pull a few clinical tricks out of my psychiatrist's bag and examine some of the dramatis personae of the Revolution as if they were patients. This would force me into empathic mode by investigating their back-grounds, rooting around in their childhoods and doing my level best to see the Revolution as they might have seen it.

I began to feel that this thing was bigger than both of us (me and whoever my 'patient' at the time was). The problem could only be put into perspective if the big picture was looked at. The Revolution was a revolution of the people and the leaders who emerged just happened to fall into place at the right time. Not only that, but the people themselves shaped the process by their collective action. I had to ask who 'the people' were, and if they were not all the people, who the people were who were not regarded as 'The People.'

The book gradually mushroomed into an investigation of the most controversial episodes of the Revolution, including the Reign of Terror, the attempt to destroy Christianity and the various violent deaths which befell both the revolutionaries and their enemies. Naturally I couldn't resist applying a few tools of my trade all along the way. I have tried to do this in as entertaining and plausible a way as possible, eschewing jargon and ensuring that whatever technical language there is will invite a more balanced perspective on a hope-lessly unbalanced historical event and throw light on the subject of revolution in general.

I have purposefully introduced section breaks into my text. My thinking, and indeed my own personal experience, is that readers can tire of absorbing large sections of prose without a mental pause. This is especially the case in the current text, where the narrative switches back and forth between historical circumstance and psychological explanation.

Acknowledgements

I wish to thank my sons Adam and Rafael who steered me gently and steadily through the digital minefield which is 21st century publishing and encouraged me to persevere. My special thanks to my wife Lesley who patiently read through innumerable drafts of the manuscript, held my hand when I lay becalmed in the Sargasso Sea of writer's block and never lost faith in my ability to return to shore with the finished product. Thanks also to my good friend Professor Bryan Lask who cast his eagle eye over the manuscript and offered me useful tips on how to tighten and brighten it. Finally, to all those friends and relatives who knew of the project from day one, thanks guys, your cheers from the sidelines meant a lot to me.

List of Illustrations

Plate section after page 72.
FRONT COVER: *The Assassination of Marat* by Jean-Joseph Weerts (1847–1927), painted circa 1880.

The author and publisher gratefully acknowledge the following for permission to reproduce copyright material:

The Execution of Louis XVI on 21ˢᵗ January 1793. The English cartoonist James Gillray captured the mood of revulsion which greeted the king's execution in a country already shaken by the violence of the Revolution. Courtesy of Pictorial Press Ltd/Alamy.

Louis XVI (1754–1793), King of France from 1774. He was devoted to his family and appalled at the prospect of shedding French blood. His weakness and vacillation fed into the forces of the Revolution which eventually destroyed him. Courtesy of World History Archive/Alamy.

An Unholy Trinity: George-Jacques Danton (1759–1794), Jean Paul Marat (1743–1793) and Maximilien de Robespierre (1758–1794). Three radical revolutionary leaders who unleashed the Terror. They have become etched into the public consciousness as either demons or heroes in a world still divided about the Revolution itself. Courtesy of The Art Archive/Alamy.

So Near and Yet So Far. Louis XVI and his family detained at Varennes near the Austrian border. Their attempted escape from France in June 1791 led to a sea-change in the public mood towards the monarchy. Courtesy of Pictorial Press Ltd/Alamy. Courtesy of PRISMA ARCHIVO/Alamy.

March of the Women on Versailles, 5ᵗʰ October 1789. Spearheaded by the market-women of Paris, an angry crowd made its way to Versailles, broke into the palace and forced the royal family to return to Paris under escort. Courtesy of The Art Archive/Alamy.

Marie Antoinette caricatured as a leopard-like beast. The royal family were often portrayed as animals or monsters. The inscription mockingly refers to the queen as the Baroness de Korff, a false identity she assumed during the flight from Paris. Courtesy of Photos 12/Alamy.

The Execution of Danton and Desmoulins on 5th April 1794. Desmoulins' childhood friendship with Robespierre gave him no immunity after his repeated attacks on Robespierre in speeches and articles. Danton's ranting eloquence at his own trial was to no avail. His last words were addressed to the executioner: 'Make sure you show my head to the people. It's worth a look.' Courtesy of FALKEN-STEINFOTO/Alamy.

Jacques Pierre Brissot (1754–1793), a leading Girondin and fervent advocate of war with Austria and Prussia as the way to save the Revolution. A bitter enemy of Robespierre, he was executed with twenty other Girondins on 31st October 1793. Courtesy of Ivan Vdovin/Alamy.

The adolescent Robespierre in the aristocratic attire which was to characterize his appearance throughout the Revolution. Courtesy of Lebrecht Music and Arts Photo Library/Alamy.

Mirror Image. Robespierre 'the Incorruptible' saw enemies everywhere, getting in the way of his ideal Revolution. Cartoon sketch copyright © Harold Behr, 2015.

The publishers apologize for any errors or omissions in the above list and would be grateful to be notified of any corrections that should be incorporated in the next edition or reprint of this book.

Chronology of the French Revolution

1789   27th–28th **April** Riot in Paris.

5th **May** The States General assembles at Versailles for the first time since 1614.

28th **May** The Third Estate begins to meet alone.

17th **June** The Third Estate assumes the title of 'The National Assembly'.

20th **June** The Third estate, locked out of its meeting place, re-assembles at a Tennis Court, where it vows not to adjourn until a new constitution is in place.

24th **June** Some nobles and clergy join with the Third Estate.

27th **June** The king orders the first two Estates to merge with the Third Estate.

11th **July** The king dismisses Necker.

14th **July** Fall of the Bastille.

16th **July** Recall of Necker.

17th **July** The king wears the revolutionary cockade at the Paris Hotel de Ville and toasts the Revolution under duress.

July–August Peasant Revolt; a wave of rumour, panic and violence spreads through the countryside ('The Great Fear').

4th–11th **August** Wave of decrees abolishing 'feudalism'.

25th **August** Declaration of Rights of Man and Citizen.

5th–6th **October** Women's march to Versailles; king is brought back to Paris.

21st **October** Martial Law decreed.

November–December Secularization of church lands and issue of Revolutionary currency.

1790   19th **June** Abolition of nobility and titles.

12th **July** Civil Constitution of Clergy, a document calling on clergy to prioritize loyalty to the state and detailing their duties and how they would be elected and paid.

14th **July** Festival of patriotic unity on the ruins of the Bastille.

27th **November** Clergy required to swear an oath of loyalty to the regime.

1791   30th **January** Mirabeau elected President of the National Assembly.

2nd **April** Death of Mirabeau.

3rd **April** Papal Bull condemns Clergy's Constitutional Oath.

18th **April** The king's aunts prevented from visiting St Cloud to say Mass with a non-juring priest.

14th **June** le Chapelier law banning workers' organizations.

20th–25th **June** The king's flight to Varennes and his ignominious return to Paris in virtual captivity.

June–July Feuillants (moderates) secede from Jacobins.

17th **July** National Guard puts down a demonstration at Champ de Mars.

27th **August** Declaration of Pillnitz: King of Prussia and Emperor of Austria call on other powers to rally to the King of France.

September Constitution of 1791 voted by Assembly.

30th **September** Dissolution of Constituent Assembly.

October Meeting of Legislative Assembly.

1792 **January** Food riots in Paris.

20th **March** Introduction of the guillotine.

20th **April** Declaration of war against Austria.

13th **June** Dismissal of Girondin ministers.

20th **June** Popular invasion of the Tuileries palace.

5th **July** Legislative Assembly states that 'the fatherland is in danger'.

20th **July** Duke of Brunswick issues a Manifesto calling on the people of France to renounce the Revolution.

10th **August** The king driven from his palace at the Tuileries, takes refuge within the assembly, is suspended.

13th **August** Royal family incarcerated in the Temple under supervision of Paris Commune.

19th **August** Lafayette, unable to persuade his army to march on Paris, joins the Austrians.

2nd **September** Verdun, strategic fortress on the road to Paris, surrenders to the Prussians.

2nd–5th **September** Massacre of prisoners in Paris prisons.

20th **September** Prussians halted at Valmy.

21st **September** First meeting of the National Convention; royalty is abolished.

6th **November** General Dumouriez defeats the Austrians at Jemappes.

11th **December** The king's trial begins with his appearance before the Convention.

1793 21st **January** Execution of the king.

1st **February** France declares war on Great Britain and the Dutch Republic.

25th–26th **February** Food riots in Paris.

7th **March** Declaration of war on Spain.

10th **March** Attempted popular insurrection in Paris; Revolutionary Tribunal set up.

March Revolt of Vendée.

5th–6th **April** General Dumouriez goes over to the Austrians; Committee of Public Safety set up.

May First Law of Maximum setting limit on grain prices; revolt at Lyons.

31ˢᵗ May–2ⁿᵈ June Girondin deputies driven from Convention.

24ᵗʰ June Adoption of the Constitution of 1793.

13ᵗʰ July Assassination of Marat.

17ᵗʰ July Remaining feudal obligations abolished without compensation.

4ᵗʰ–5ᵗʰ September Popular insurrection in Paris; beginning of Terror.

17ᵗʰ September Law of Suspects: all suspected of counter-revolution to be held in custody.

29ᵗʰ September Law of General Maximum putting ceiling on food prices and wages.

10ᵗʰ October Constitution declared suspended until end of war.

October Lyons revolt suppressed; 'de-Christianizing' campaign.

16ᵗʰ October Marie Antoinette executed.

31ˢᵗ October Execution of Girondins.

4ᵗʰ December Revolutionary government established.

1794 **26ᵗʰ February–3ʳᵈ March** Laws of Ventôse: suspects' goods sequestrated and distributed to the needy.

15ᵗʰ March Arrest of Hébertists.

25ᵗʰ March Execution of Hébertists.

30ᵗʰ–31 March Arrest of Dantonists.

5ᵗʰ April Execution of Danton and Desmoulins.

7ᵗʰ May The Convention recognizes the existence of the Supreme Being.

8ᵗʰ June Festival of the Supreme Being.

10ᵗʰ June Law of 22ⁿᵈ Prairial inaugurating the Great Terror: defence lawyers and witnesses dispensed with.

May–June Affair of Catherine Théot, cult leader protected by Robespierre.

26ᵗʰ June Austrians defeated at Battle of Fleurus.

26ᵗʰ–29ᵗʰ July Crisis of Thermidor; fall of Robespierre.

28ᵗʰ July Robespierre executed.

1ˢᵗ August Law of 22ⁿᵈ Prairial repealed.

12ᵗʰ November Jacobin Club in Paris closed.

24ᵗʰ December Repeal of Maximum laws.

Theoretical Preamble

'History is a nightmare from which I am trying to awake.'
James Joyce ('Proteus')

If James Joyce is to be taken seriously, history is at once a mix of frightening fantasy and grim reality. There is an implicit warning in this that we must try to make sense of the past if we want to avoid a tragic outcome. The same thought was echoed by the Mexican philosopher Santayana: 'Those who do not understand their past are doomed to repeat it', was his lugubrious prophecy and Freud took up the idea and planted it at the centre of his treatment method.

According to psychoanalysis destructive actions can be averted by embarking on a therapeutic journey which involves the retrieval of aspects of the past which have previously lain outside of our conscious awareness. The insight which we gain in this way can re-direct us into more creative channels. Group analysts argue that the same principle applies to our collective past. Group memories, often distorted into myths, steer us into destructive conflicts which only muddy the waters further and make it more difficult to hold on to rational judgments about the way forward.

The past can be viewed with scientific objectivity but it is also coloured by our passions, which cannot be ignored. The vast ocean of facts on which we bob around (scientists might refer to this as the raw data of our research) requires a modicum of selectivity and this is subjectively determined according to our tastes and fancies. Our field of study has to be circumscribed. In other words, the ocean has to have a net thrown into it if new life forms are to be discovered.

My trawl through the history of the French Revolution has taken place in well fished waters. The new forms of life which I am seeking are the thought processes (both individual and group) of those who lived through those perilous times. All researchers should have at least one question which they would like answered by their research. My question is: Can we draw any inferences about today's revolutionary movements from the emotions, thoughts, visions and actions of the people who were caught up in that first major European revolution over two centuries ago? A subsidiary question could be: From our knowledge of how people behaved then can we work towards better political solutions for the societies of the future?

Although I have drawn on psychology to write this book, I do not think of the book as a 'psychohistory' of the Revolution. Psychohistory is a hybrid concept which implies that there is such a thing as 'pure' history, a narrative which can be told shorn of its psychological context. Instead, I like what Peter Gay has to say about the relationship between history and psychology:

> The professional historian has always been a psychologist – an amateur psychologist. Whether he knows it or not, he operates within a theory of human nature; he attributes motives, studies passions, analyses irrationality and constructs his work on the tacit conviction that human beings display certain stable and discernible traits, certain predictable, or at least discoverable modes of coping with their experience. He discovers causes, and his discovery normally includes acts of the mind.

In writing this book I have subscribed to what Arthur Miller has called 'a unified concept of human beings, the intimate psychological side joined with the social-political' (A. Miller, *Timebends*, p. 587). This corresponds to the holistic approach to the study of mankind which gained currency in the early twentieth century (K. Goldstein), a philosophy which integrates the study of brain function, group dynamics, individual psychology and interpersonal relationships. Each new branch of science introduces fresh concepts wrought in its own new language, contributions which can be seen either as bricks to a tower of Babel or, as I believe, a panorama of fascinating architectural designs enhancing the landscape.

Floating above the world of psychological science are the philosophers and the artists, whose insights into the fundamental problems of existence sometimes trump those of the scientists. Psychologically minded historians are free to draw from any of these sources if they feel that in so doing they can enliven the story of their chosen topic (in this case the French Revolution) and shed light on some of its mysteries.

There is a paradox inherent in the French Revolution. Two contradictory forces emerged side by side and fed into each other – the thinking of the Enlightenment, a product of man's evolving intellect, co-existed compatibly with an upsurge of rage driven essentially by man's animal instincts. This apparent contradiction has to be understood if we are to make sense of the violence which swept away so many people and institutions.

The violence of the Revolution swirled around two symbols of leadership, the king and the people. Each represented a fundamentally different concept of power, one descending from above, the other emanating from below, from the grass roots as it were. The symbol of monarchy, the king, was bolstered by the people's belief in religion, but the philosophers of the Enlightenment were discovering new ideas for governing society based on reason, not faith.

There was a convergence of sympathies between those who believed that the future lay in their own hands and those who felt the pangs of physical suffering but lacked the intellectual wherewithal to articulate their frustrations. The Revolution began when the two forces intermingled and translated their shared ideas into action. Violence in the cause of a better society became an integral part of the revolutionary philosophy.

Those who believed that the two concepts, power gained from on high and power gained from the masses could be knitted together into a single harmonious fabric were eventually swept away by the tide of violence and replaced by leaders whose voices resonated with factions which believed in the supremacy of the one and the extinction of the other.

The Revolution spawned a crop of paranoid leaders, which is not surprising. Any revolution basically opens up a split in society which invites violent projections of badness into others who are then denounced as enemies. Lines of battle were drawn between those who stood for and against revolutionary change. Compromise and moderation were tainted by the stigma of betrayal. As the Revolution rolled on further splits arose, resulting in political groups becoming more tightly knit, smaller in size, more ferocious in temper and more fervent about the rightness of their principles.

In our tour of the revolutionary mind-set we will investigate how paranoia feeds on itself until power is lost and destruction looms. Paranoia is based on a dream of perfection which cannot be realized. The paranoid leader is also grandiose and power-hungry. When he fails to kill his enemy and his dream collapses he is faced with only one choice: suicide. The man who epitomized the collapse of his dream of the perfect society and his failure to destroy the enemies who surrounded him in increasing numbers was Robespierre. We will be looking at his childhood to see whether we can discover the roots of his idealism and its malignant transformation into destructiveness.

Another form of grandiosity which also ended in the death of the leader is to be found in Danton. His life is an example of how a foible which might have been regarded as innocent, even laudable in a time of peace, became enlarged to monstrous proportions during the Revolution until it literally tore him apart. In Danton's case his two-faced dalliance with both royalty and the mob proved his undoing.

Danton and Robespierre were opposites. Danton was coarse, warm-blooded, and opportunistic. Robespierre, the 'sea-green incorruptible', was prissy, principled and unforgiving. In the storm that was the Revolution they could not stand together but nor could they command a following apart from each other. The Revolution devoured them both.

Groups tend to find leaders who match their needs. A paranoid group seeks out a paranoid leader, (Hitler is the prime example), someone who splits the world into good and evil. Conversely, a leader inspired by a vision of unity (Mandela is the modern exemplar) brings the group together. The difference between these two leaders is that the one saw 'bad' in others, the other saw 'good' in all, both the 'self' group and the 'other' group alike.

In the French Revolution the chaos and drift of the revolutionary movement complicated the picture. There was hope and idealism on the one hand, anger and despair on the other. These emotions in different combinations pervaded all the leaders who rose and fell from power. The changing leadership mirrored the rapidly fluctuating needs and moods of the group.

There is a bond between leader and group as complex as that which exists between parent and child. The leader is born out of the group and comes to represent the future. A group in trouble, a group which experiences itself as being in need of rescue or revival, may invest the 'new-born' leader with messianic properties; a group which experiences itself as harbouring destructive forces within it may lay the blame for failing to rid the group of its badness on the leader and set in motion a dynamic of expulsion. A leader who is experienced as having been foisted on the group from above, as was Louis XVI, the absolute monarch, is cast as an alien being and sacrificed as a scapegoat.

Hatred lay at the heart of revolutionary violence. The knife with which Charlotte Corday pierced the chest of Marat was driven by her hatred of the man whom she perceived to be a monster. Her dream was to save France, but the immediate aftermath was that her act dragged others to their deaths without stemming the Reign of Terror. The episode which ended in the trial and execution of Charlotte Corday tell us about the virtues and failings of self-sacrifice. Marat and Corday now live on in the public imagination as a macabre couple, mainly through iconic paintings – Marat the saintly corpse in his bathtub and Corday the tall, beautiful, dignified woman defiant in the face of her captors. The case helps us to think about the role of murder in a murderous social context and we may well wonder whether to enter a plea of mitigation in such instances.

The closer we get to the minds of perpetrators and victims the more we have the need for a psychiatric perspective. It is possible to plan a murderous act in a lucid frame of mind and repress all compassionate and conflictual thoughts at the same time. Could this be what psychiatrists call 'la belle indifference', a dissociative denial of painful reality that nevertheless enables purposive acts to be performed? There is a diagnostic complexity about a detached mind-set which readies the person for murder and self-sacrifice in what they believe to be a noble cause. Terms like 'delusional', 'paranoid' and 'grandiose' fall short of encompassing the whole picture, but nor can they be entirely dispensed with when the social context offers us tens of thousands of people with similar mind-sets.

Groups as well as individuals can be paranoid in the sense of exaggerating a potential menace from the outside. Like individuals, groups can be inflated by a false sense of their own power. Exactly when a group belief crosses a line into unreality is a matter that should interest not only psychiatrists but philosophers and all students of group behaviour. Regardless of the passage of time, the truth only comes more sharply into focus when we apply our current knowledge of the workings of the human mind to the events of yesteryear.

Metaphor is a way of lifting people into a state of greater mindfulness. Without metaphor we are left with an arid technical language ruled entirely by the tyranny of logic. Metaphors imbue our lives with meaning. Their ambiguity colours our language and signposts various possibilities for changing our understanding. Yesterday's metaphor crystallizes into today's new idea. The fact that there is more than one way of looking at something leads us away from the worship of monoliths.

The age-old problem is that more than one perspective opens the way to dispute. When the potential for conflict arises, synthesis and antithesis do not always lead to thesis. Without reflection it is all too easy for conflict and violence to become conflated. The subtle difference between them is lost on a slippery slope towards impulsive action. One of humanity's encrusted problems is how (indeed, whether) groups and communities can resolve their differences without falling on each other, especially when bodily pangs of hunger, fear, lust, rage and greed rise to dominate our consciousness. Driven by the cravings of the body, we are constantly striving to escape from the snarling animal in us.

In our travels through the history of the Revolution we find ourselves spiritually uplifted at one moment by noble rhetoric, then plunged unexpectedly into the chill waters of persecution with all its attendant forms of brutality. The political idealists who dreamt of a utopia were at the same time plotting to destroy each other and were swept away in an orgy of bloodshed. Surely there is something wrong here, some basic fault in the workings of the mind which, in one breath calls us to the heights of altruism, at the same time threatening to fling us against each other in bloody conflict.

Our agenda must therefore entertain the question: How is it that the impulse to commit violence can co-exist in the same mind as the impulse to foster altruism? Our history of the Revolution provides examples of the sort of skewed thinking which justified murder in the name of the good society. Leading the way was the paragon of revolutionary virtue, Maximilien Robespierre, whose ticket for utopia took France through hell and who was doomed never to reach his destination.

In psychological terms, we are looking at the twin phenomenon of idealization and denigration. Those who set out to follow their dream of perfection, considering themselves pure in mind as Robespierre did, sooner or later find themselves stumbling into a lethal battle with those who do not share their particular view of goodness. Idealism, the embrace of 'good', is stalked by its ugly twin, a creature who stubbornly insists on a different version of goodness. If the two views differ ever so slightly, the chances are that blood will boil and eventually be shed.

We learn about ourselves from the reactions of others, a process which starts in infancy, when parents mirror the baby's emerging gestures with demonstrations of pleasure and love, setting in motion a benign cycle of warmth, intimacy and self-confidence. But the process can also be negative. Repeated failure to acknowledge the baby's attempts at engagement, or misunderstanding of the baby's cues, can be frightening and discouraging, leading to assumptions that the world is a hostile place and that others cannot be trusted. Parents who are unable to hold up an approving mirror for the child to gaze into create an emotional climate of wariness and withdrawal.

As the child matures adult constructs are put in place to harmonize with childhood perceptions. Strangers, and even familiar others, can take on menacing proportions and the self is experienced as coming under threat. Comfort, companionship and conspiracy are sought with those who most resemble the self, until a group self emerges which feels strong enough to withstand the sinister forces in the outside world.

In politics, any sudden, dramatic process which sharply divides people into positions of being 'for' and 'against' something sets in motion a process of crude generalization in which people and groups are swept willy-nilly into either 'good' and 'bad' camps. A ranting demagogue stirs the passions, making it difficult for other views to be heard. In the process the voice of moderation is stilled.

Hubert Humphrey, Democratic candidate in the 1968 United States presidential election, remembers the era of the McCarthy witch-hunts like this:

> The language of the time, the rhetoric of extremes, had the awful consequence of forcing almost all of us into simplistic positions.
>
> When everything we did in relation to the Communists was attacked as evil, bad, wrong, there was little room to respond, "Yes but . . . " To be heard, the rhetoric in response required claims just as simplistic: our policies were noble, sound and perfect.
>
> Government is much more complex, and in times of rapid change, when empires are tumbling, social orders disintegrating, and value systems changing, and it is very difficult to be precise in what you see and what you know.

Humphrey's experience helps us to understand the need for simplification during a crisis. There is no time for reflection or elaboration during a crisis. Rather, a sense of urgency impels the truncation of language to a minimum. The message has to be got across as swiftly as possible and fleshed out as emotionally as possible. In the process, facts are distorted or even discarded and their place taken by the language of wish-fulfilment and fear-mongering.

The French Revolution was a crisis which spilled over into the rest of Europe. After centuries of stasis the political landscape began to shift with terrifying rapidity. Ancient structures started to crack and no one could be sure from which direction the tremor was coming or in which direction it was heading. Those who believed in their own power to control such elemental forces resorted to the language of over-simplification, appropriating it from its religious authorship and spiriting it into the political arena of discourse.

The disembodied qualities of goodness and badness were inevitably located in symbols which carried an emotional charge. A person, very often the group leader, came to acquire symbolic significance as a hero or saint. The person and the symbol became confused in the popular mind. Heroes became villains overnight and there was traffic in the reverse direction too. As with individuals, so too with institutions. Good was pitted against evil, right against wrong, purity and austerity against corruption and excess. The leaders of the Revolution fleshed out stark contrasts with over-simplified images – emblems of nature, symbols of rebirth and myths of ancient struggles against tyranny which could rouse the passions of the people.

During the Revolution the ranks of conservatism had little with which to counter such imagery beyond an appeal to the drooping flags of royalty, the dead statues of past figures and the hollow rituals of church worship. Both the aristocracy and the Catholic church had lost their moral authority and with it their capacity for inspiring identification with the resentful populace.

The dynamic forces shaping adult relationships take their cue from a template laid down by family relationships. Authority, nurture, power, love and hate permeate attachments which stem from parent, sibling and couple relationships. These are then transmuted into social and work relationships. Through the mists of time we can deduce that a massive upheaval like the French Revolution would have brought out qualities in some which set them up as leaders when they would otherwise have been consigned to obscurity. The antecedents of leadership qualities can be traced to the earliest interpersonal experiences in which the sense of self is defined against close attachment figures in the family.

Unfortunately, the opportunity of probing the psyches of our bewigged or unkempt subjects from the end of the eighteenth century is lost forever, but we can still plough through a mountain of indirect evidence about their public and intimate lives to arrive at some safe conclusions about their motives and personalities. We can make inferences from Robespierre's childhood attachments and losses to his passionate embrace of the Revolution and from Louis XVI's emotionally deprived upbringing to his depressed, passive and religiose tendencies in later life. A picture, once caricatured, can be re-drawn and shaded in.

The 'other' does not have to be a person. The plasticity of the human mind enables us to form relationships with abstract entities – groups, ideologies or philosophies. In 1789 the ties that bound people to objects representing these abstractions (the tricolor or a religious icon for example,) formed attachments as powerful as any that might exist between creatures of flesh-and-blood.

The revolutionary identity borrowed a leaf from ancient Greece and Rome. Some revolutionaries were so immersed in stories of martyrs and warriors who stood against tyrants that they took on the identities of these ancient characters and like infatuated adolescents turned them into heroes. The rhetoric which once roused the citizens of antiquity in the market-place rang out again during the French Revolution.

Stories told and retold become cultural myths. They are neither fact nor fiction but an emotional blend of both. Myths are designed to hold groups together in a shared identification with a common past. The ability to construct myths is both a blessing and a curse. Led by mythical prompts we are able to project ourselves into the future and build stories which can be a source of hope but also conflict.

If a myth is built out of a traumatic experience, the characters who people the myth take on the roles of victims and perpetrators of the trauma, shaped by time and emotion into allies and enemies. Fresh conflict arises when groups with different mythical legacies choose to re-enact their myths in a culturally driven attempt to right wrongs. If contradictory myths are allowed to unfold unchecked by reason or empathy the task of reconciling the contradictions becomes harder.

This is where historians come into their own. By scrutinizing myths, recognizing their cultural importance, toning down some of their distortions and carefully re-arranging some of their architecture into a less stereotyped format, the historian takes a step closer to the reconciliation of conflict which is at the heart of all civilized behaviour. The keynote of reconciliation is truth, as the South African experience of the 1990s has shown. In order for the truth to emerge, a story has to be told again and again in a setting which is as free of inflammation and recrimination as possible.

Wounds have to be healed, a process which involves grief, pain and anger. It does not matter that the people who tell the story may be many generations away from the traumatic event. Trauma has its own self-perpetuating aftermath, and the myths surrounding a traumatic event take on a life of their own. The historian is like a psychotherapist, a person who listens to the tales of the past and then ventures to reflect them back to the teller in softer colours and against a broader background.

The divide which separates groups brewing in a state of mutual hostility can be thought of as a psychological split in the body politic. The precursor of such a split is a psychic device known as projection, a hurling towards 'the enemy' of negative traits. Each party blames the other for mishaps, disasters and tragedies while disowning responsibility for any of these.

Whenever there is talk of enemies the term 'paranoia' comes readily to mind. The paranoid individual may not be completely out of touch with reality, ('they' may actually be out to get him), but when we try to dissect out reality from fantasy we move imperceptibly into the domain of psychiatry where fear and suspicion dominate thinking and cloud judgment.

We can distribute all the leaders of the Revolution along a spectrum of paranoia and it is difficult to draw the line between normality and pathology, especially when the term paranoia lends itself not only to individual but collective behaviour. Paranoia is an infectious state of mind, closely related to panic and hysteria. All signify the trampling of doubt into certainty. Those events which strike fear into the heart – famine, disease and violence – send shock waves through the mind impelling it into a state from which reflection and reasoning vanish. Survival is the keynote of such a frame of mind which in its worst form steels itself against the possibility of annihilation by plotting to annihilate others.

Destruction is only one half of the picture. As human beings we depend on each other, not only for brute survival but for civilized advancement through the acquisition of knowledge. Information gathered from our predecessors is spread, concentrated and stored. While this is happening there is a parallel process of attrition and decay taking place. Just as individuals live and die, so do groups, even whole civilizations, come and go.

The philosopher and sociologist Norbert Elias was one of the first to grasp this particular nettle. He gave us the concept of 'figuration', a notion which describes the interconnectedness of human existence throughout the life cycle. Elias had the idea that people are interdependent with others from across the generations, including ancestors whom they would never have met except through stories told within families and groups. Throwing a time-line into the distant past he has shown how our psychological make-up has been moulded by certain social and cultural groupings in both past and present. It is the process of knowing our ancestors that has made us more aware of how we resemble them but also how we differ from them.

According to Elias, we exist as networks of interdependent human beings, bonded together in relationships based on a dynamic tension between closeness and distance. (Mennell p. 254). The more differentiated the group, the more complex are its functions. Individuals within the group assume roles which articulate with those of other individuals in a more or less organized fashion. One of these roles is that of leadership, a role which confers power on some individuals whose task is to stabilize and protect the group.

Power is an essential component of group life. It is a dynamic entity with fluid properties. It can drain away from one part of the group network into another or it can solidify, tightening its hold on the group to a point where tension causes the bonds holding the group together to rupture. The French Revolution was an explosion caused by the snapping and tearing of bonds of power which had become impossibly tight. The ancient rituals of the aristocracy had become hollow, useless and stultifying.

The French Revolution began as a revolution of the nobles against the king. In the court of Versailles it was important for the king to dominate the nobles. The activities of the court were tightly controlled by elaborate rituals and rules of etiquette. Everyone had his place. Elias explains why the activities of the court at Versailles were so dominated by ceremony, etiquette and ritual. Each noble was tightly interlaced with other nobles at court in a calibrated relationship with every other noble along a power continuum. The web of interrelationships determined status and prestige. The most powerful members of the nobility, with the king at the top, were constrained by a mesh of rituals as tight as metallic bands. Movement became virtually impossible, short of an explosion. Through our knowledge of the past, shaped by both memory and myth, we can begin to think futuristically. We can start to predict the effect that we might have on societies of the future and we can sharpen our ability to identify with others. Over the centuries our growing self-knowledge has also allowed us to become more capable of predicting how others might react towards us. With greater self-knowledge has come a broader range of emotions including the ability to empathize with others, to experience shame and to take responsibility for our own acts.

CHAPTER ONE

Louis XVI
The Scapegoat King

*'It is to the family of the Capets that the French people owe
all the evils under the weight of which they have
groaned for so many centuries.'*
Public prosecutor at the trial of Madame Elisabeth,
sister of Louis XVI

One definition of a family is that it is a group of people related by blood or marriage. Another is that it comprises all the descendants of a common ancestor. Louis XVI was cursed by both these definitions. By a great irony he was the mildest, most humane, least acquisitive member of the Bourbon family to rule France since Henri IV, the great peacemaker and religious reformer whose reign ended with his assassination in 1610. Louis' tragedy was that he was made a scapegoat for the oppression, injustice and barbaric cruelty inflicted on the people of France under the reign of the Bourbons who followed Henri.

He was a sickly, shy, strangely silent child with an obsessional cast of mind and a preference for solitary pastimes, the odd one out among his siblings. His two younger brothers, destined to outlive him and become kings of France in the post-Napoleonic era, looked on him with contempt. He only grew in confidence during his early teenage years when he was introduced to the pleasures of riding and hunting. He never lost his disquieting reticence, though, which was reinforced by tutors who emphasized that reserve and restraint, the qualities of *retenue,* were essential royal attributes.

His slowness, apathy and reticence meant that he was often thought dull, but he was by no means unintelligent. He showed a talent for mathematics, physics and astronomy, enjoyed history and geography – especially map-reading – and had a fascination for gadgetry. Had he lived today he would probably have been placed somewhere along the milder end of the autistic spectrum. His aptitude for repairing clocks and locks would have served him well as a career in another life. His role as dauphin, however, would not allow him to lead the life of a social isolate. He would have to marry and conduct affairs of state. When the deaths of his father and older brothers earmarked him for the throne he grew close to his grandfather, Louis XV, who reluctantly took on the task of grooming him for the heavy burdens of kingship. But he showed no interest in politics or philosophy. His greatest social handicap was his embarrassing tendency to be silent beyond the dictates of kingly reserve. His greatest political handicap was his paralyzing indecisiveness.

He had an unfortunate social presence, too. He was ponderous both in build and manner and is described as walking with a waddle. His social graces were not improved by his tendency to fall asleep in council meetings and church services. His portraits show a lugubrious expression which probably reflected his depressed state of mind. There is certainly enough evidence to support the view that he was depressed. He had been raised in an emotionally barren environment, the recipient of little love from parents, whom he hardly saw apart from ceremonial occasions. His mother died when he was eleven, his father soon afterwards. An adored older brother had died when Louis was seven years old, deflecting his attachment onto a sister who stayed close to him through the tribulations that were in store.

His constant sadness and bouts of grief were visible to all, but gained him little sympathy. He lavished tender love on his own children, and suffered at the deaths of his first two children in infancy, and that of his firstborn son at the age of seven, a sensitive child whose death from tuberculosis of the spine ended a long period of agony over his frailty and the deformities caused by his illness. The child's terminal decline coincided with the opening of the States General in 1789. Louis and his wife were already the objects of hatred and abuse which intruded into their grief and would continue unremittingly until their deaths.

He was benevolent and compassionate by nature, and he wanted at all costs to avoid confrontation. These were virtues which would have won him favour in peaceful times, but they worked against him when what was needed was inspired leadership and the ability to fight fire with fire. When the violence of the Revolution reached the doors of his palace he reacted outwardly with accommodating behaviour, while inwardly he became devious and obstructive. The safety of his family and the avoidance of bloodshed were paramount in his eyes. His own fate did not matter. Underlying his phlegmatic disposition was a selflessness strengthened by a deep commitment to his Catholic faith.

The tendency for groups to appoint a carrier for their own badness and then set about getting rid of that carrier is as old as the human species. It rests on the magical belief that badness can be purged from the community if it is projected into a creature, person or group within the community perceived as responsible for introducing it. The culprit or culprits can then be expelled from the group along with the badness and the group restored to its pristine condition. The original goat from the bible was crowned with a wreath of thorns and at first simply driven out into the desert, but because the silly animal tended to wander back into the community the process had to be taken a step further by pushing it off a cliff.

History is replete with accounts of persecution culminating in atrocities, wars and centuries-long hatred between groups, all founded on the myth of the scapegoat, in which the blameless are blamed and the innocent pronounced guilty. However, the woes of the group are never alleviated by this device. The relief obtained by the expulsion or death of the victim is usually short-lived. The underlying causes remain firmly in place, the problem invariably recurs, impelling the group to find a new scapegoat, and the cycle is repeated.

Eighteenth-century France was susceptible to this myth. Its people had suffered centuries of hardship and decades of sustained warfare. Cultural myths of traumas dating back to antiquity had been kept alive and stored in the nation's social memory. These myths rose to the surface when the country faced economic decline and the threat of starvation. In a replay of ancient legends, heroes were brought to life who had once rescued the country from monsters and tyrants.

In small groups the person chosen for the part of monster or scapegoat sometimes plays an active part in the process by behaving in a way which offends the mores of the group. In a country of twenty-six million people, however, the personal attributes of the intended scapegoats scarcely mattered. Louis and his family took on an almost entirely representational role. It was enough that they were perceived as having malign power and experienced as alien to the people amongst whom they lived.

Louis inherited the throne on a wave of optimism and only came slowly into his role as scapegoat. His grandfather, Louis XV, would have been a more deserving candidate. He had done nothing to reform the monarchy or rescue France from its economic troubles. An attempt to assassinate him in 1757 led to the public torture and execution of the would-be assassin, a feeble-minded servant called Damiens, providing a spectacle which caused widespread revulsion. This and other cruel punishments perpetrated during the reign of Louis XV imprinted themselves on the collective consciousness of France and highlighted the brutality of the regime. Satirists like Voltaire and philosophers like Rousseau provided the intellectual ammunition for an assault on the barbaric traditions which had produced such cruelty. They and many other thinkers of the Enlightenment painted the picture of a new era based on reason and freedom from oppression. Louis XV's death in 1774 from smallpox was hardly mourned, and hope was in the air that the new young king would bring France out of the dark ages.

This hope proved illusory. Louis XVI was well intentioned, but he was hopelessly miscast as king. His attempts to reform France were thwarted at every step of the way by the self-aggrandizing nobles who surrounded him, and his offer of help to the American rebels in their war of independence against the British brought France to the edge of bankruptcy. The country could not be rescued by the tinkering of his economic advisers, who were in any case hamstrung by the aristocratic opposition to change. The slide from hope into disappointment created a mood of fury and blame which settled on the head of the one person with symbolic responsibility for the country's troubles, the king.

But there is a paradox in seeing Louis entirely as a victim. He exercised real power as a monarch, and this has to be differentiated from the magical powers projected onto him by those who believed in his divine powers and the majority who believed in the inherent tyranny of Bourbon rule. We must ask to what extent Louis was capable of influencing the situation he found himself in by the exercise of his power, and what part his personal attributes played in his appointment as a scapegoat of the Revolution.

The arrival on the scene of his bride-to-be provided an added dimension to the scapegoat myth. Marie Antoinette was the daughter of the Empress Maria Theresa of Austria, a country which had been involved in a long and debilitating war with France, the wounds of which had not healed. The machinations of the two royal houses to bring about an arranged marriage between the fifteen year old dauphin and the fourteen year old Austrian princess as a means of sealing the new Franco-Austrian alliance took no account of the sentiments in France towards an enemy which had caused grievous destruction and loss of life. The image of the evil Bourbon king was now merged with that of his foreign wife, the daughter of France's greatest enemy.

Tyranny and foreignness had come together in the minds of the French people, creating the perfect conditions for turning the royal couple into a two-headed monster destined for the role of scapegoat.

The reality of their lives as a couple was a different story. In the tradition of politically arranged marriages, Louis had had no say over the choice of his bride. To the exasperation of France's elder statesmen he showed the same indifference towards his young wife as he did to the world of politics. As husband and wife they were wretchedly incompatible. Louis was lacking in charm, wit and elegance, Marie Antoinette was spirited, feisty and gregarious. She enjoyed dancing, frolicking in amateur theatricals and indulging in social intrigues, tastes which held no interest whatsoever for her ungainly and emotionally inert husband.

For the first six years of the couple's marriage their sex life was impaired, not only by Louis' lack of libido but by a physical problem affecting the royal phallus. Louis suffered from phimosis, a tight band of tissue around the prepuce which interferes with erection. He balked at the minor operation required to correct this, but the fate of the Bourbon dynasty depended on his dependant organ, and he apparently submitted to the surgeon's knife, although there is no documented evidence to this effect. The couple proved fertile, but the fact that their first child was a girl sent a further ripple of anxiety through the court. Then two sons were born, and the future of the line seemed to have been secured. A year later a fourth child was born, a girl, who died shortly before her first birthday.

The fears of the people widened the gulf between fantasy and reality. The royal couple were turned into caricatures of themselves, the realities of their lives into grotesque myths. Their faults and weaknesses were seized upon and enlarged, their virtues and strengths obliterated.

Before the two-headed Bourbon monster could be made into a scapegoat, it had to be stripped of its power. This task appeared formidable. The beast was perceived as having tentacles everywhere in the form of laws, institutions, traditions, customs and even thoughts, which though outwardly innocent, concealed the monster's evil intentions. The first stage in the dismemberment of the monster came in the form of attacks with words and images. The royal couple were subjected to insults and obscenities thrown at them through every medium. Pamphlets, newspapers, cartoons, songs and theatrical productions outdid one another in their malicious and pornographic representations.

Louis was turned into a cuckold and depicted as a donkey or a pig. Marie Antoinette was portrayed as a sexual predator, shown in embraces with men and women alike and compared with the notorious women of antiquity. Her extravagant lifestyle was rendered into a monstrous crime deserving of the death penalty. These journalistic and artistic outpourings were accompanied by a chorus of verbal abuse which greeted the couple at their public appearances. Louis and Marie were shaken by the intensity of the hatred, but whereas Louis was more inclined to react with mournful resignation, Marie Antoinette developed a steely hatred, and threw herself into intrigues with her Austrian relatives, exhorting them to act in order to alleviate the family's dire situation.

The attacks on Marie Antoinette exceeded in venom those on Louis. She was doubly a monster, partly because of her foreignness – a popular epithet was *'l'Austrichienne'* ('the Austrian bitch') – but even more because she was a woman. Deeper emotions were at work in which the despair of a people who had suffered hunger, oppression and injustice was rooted in a frustrated longing to be fed and comforted by a loving mother. When these needs could not be met in reality the nation sought out a symbolic mother in whom they could invest hope that their suffering would cease. The new world promised to them by the Revolution, a society of freedom and plenty, was this Good Mother, the personification of the biblical land flowing with milk and honey. This was the mother who would love them unconditionally and assuage their hunger. In the shadows was the image of Marie Antoinette as the Bad Mother, a woman who had withheld her love and her milk and turned her affections elsewhere to gratify her own base instincts. Their murderous rage at this abandonment and betrayal knew no bounds.

By the same token Louis was the father who had failed them. In his impotence he had neither protected them from the cruelty of his forebears, nor that of his wife and her nefarious associates, for whose tyrannical rule he, as king, was responsible. In the recesses of the collective mind he too must be destroyed and replaced by a new father, a government by the people, who could assume their own authority through their elected representatives. In tandem with these primitively driven attacks came a barrage of reasoned arguments against the monarchy as a concept, spearheaded by the *philosophes* and amalgamated into an ideology by the new breed of politicians, many of them lawyers, who now made up the body politic. This two-pronged attack by the combined forces of emotion and reason surrounded the royal couple in a pincer movement from which there was no escape.

═ ❖ ═

An outpouring of projections turned Louis and his wife into a combined bad object which grew into a monster. After the monster had been exposed to the public gaze it had to be tamed, which meant that it had to be brought under the control of the people. This meant driving it out of its familiar habitat and conveying it to a more restricted one, where it could be kept under scrutiny. The Revolution had begun with a mighty surge to what was then regarded as the centre of the nation, the royal court at Versailles. But the deputies of 1789 soon designated this a false centre, an excrescence created by the sun king to escape the noxious vapours of Paris. The true centre, they believed, now lay with the citizens of Paris, and it was to Paris that Louis, still the nominal leader of his people, would have to go.

In October 1789 a large crowd, consisting mostly of market women angry at the hardships imposed on the country by the latest food shortages and price rises, set out on a march to confront the king at Versailles. The cry for bread soon changed to a demand for the royal family to come to Paris. A delegation from the crowd invaded the palace, haranguing the king and terrifying the queen, who hid with her children in an inner recess.

True to character, Louis attempted to placate the crowd and took the advice of his frightened troop commander that the situation would become untenable unless he acceded to the crowd's demand. So it was that the royal family, surrounded by a triumphant and jeering crowd, set out on the first of their humiliating coach journeys to take up residence in the disused palace of the Tuileries. Now there was only one centre of power in France, Paris. The monster had proved tamer than expected. For a brief moment it seemed that he might even provide the nation with the bread that was desperately needed. Among the jeers that accompanied the royal coach could be heard the chant that 'the baker, the baker's wife and the baker's boy' had been taken.

The sequence of attacks by which the royal couple were robbed of their status, dignity, humanity and ultimately their lives is a familiar scapegoating sequence. First came the war of words, the distortions of their image in the public mind and their subjection to humiliating acts which acknowledged the new trappings of the Revolution. Louis colluded with this by displaying himself wearing the revolutionary bonnet. He was stripped of his Bourbon identity and renamed Citizen Capet, after the man from whom the Bourbon dynasty had sprung. The acts which limited his power and freedom of movement followed hard on the heels these humiliations. The final act saw his imprisonment, trial and execution.

Between July 1789 and June 1791 the enfeebled monster was prodded into a corner by laws which limited its powers. Louis had allowed himself to be dragged along by the revolutionary tide. He was still the king and there were many, including Robespierre, who thought it possible to advance the course of the Revolution within the framework of a constitutional monarchy. But there were already strident voices calling for a republic, and there would come a time when Louis, egged on by his queen, would decide that enough was enough.

Of all the indignities and restrictions imposed on him, the one that caused him the greatest distress was the attack on his beloved Catholic church. He had allowed the revolutionaries to strip the church of its wealth; he had been helpless in the face of a law forcing clergy to take an oath of loyalty to the state; but his pious nature rebelled when he discovered that he and his family would no longer be allowed to say mass conducted by priests who had not taken the oath of allegiance to the Revolution. When this fresh insult dawned on him, the indecisive monarch decided that the time had come for him and his family to leave France. The monster was about to surprise his captors and break free from captivity.

Towards midnight on 20th June 1791, a portly figure wearing a grey wig walked unnoticed out of the palace of the Tuileries and climbed heavily into a waiting carriage. This was Louis, disguised as one of his financial advisers, a man of similar build. After an anxious wait he was joined by his flustered queen. Marie Antoinette had left the palace separately, lost her bearings and blundered around in the dark for a precious half-hour before locating the getaway carriage.

The king's sister Madame Elisabeth, the five-year-old dauphin, dressed as a girl and his twelve year old sister were already seated in the carriage. If stopped, they would present themselves, with forged documents at the ready, as the entourage of a German baroness, a part played by the children's governess, Madame de Tourzel. Louis was to be her valet and Marie Antoinette the children's governess.

The carriage wove a circuitous route to the outskirts of Paris where the royal party climbed into another, more spacious, carriage, loaded to the gills with food and luxury commodities. This carriage was not only conspicuous, it was drawn by a large team of horses who would need to be refreshed and replaced along the way. The night before, one of the king's younger brothers, showing infinitely more good sense, had set out for the border in a light two-wheeler drawn by one horse. But the royal couple had not wanted the family to be separated, so one large carriage it had to be.

The royal family had already had several terrifying experiences at the hands of ugly crowds, yet they still retained a magical belief in their own immunity. Louis was impervious to the risks of being overtaken or identified along the way. Far from being perturbed, he was excited by the idea of travelling through his realm, like a child on a big adventure. He eagerly traced the route on his map, pointing out interesting landmarks to his family. With the same childlike innocence, he poked his head out of the carriage to greet passers by and climbed out at staging posts to pass the time of day with local townsfolk. Before the royal family had gone far, their identity was an open secret.

Despite a combination of mishap and foolishness, they nearly made it. Late on the night of the 21st June the carriage lumbered into the small town of Varennes, a few miles from the border. But events had overtaken them. Loyal troops waiting to escort them to safety had given up on their arrival and disbanded for the night. Meantime the alarm had been sounded in Paris and fast-riding horsemen had set off in pursuit of the suspicious-looking carriage. These were followed by couriers from the National Assembly armed with the authority to detain the royal family.

Further along the route a postmaster who was sure that he recognized the king had galloped ahead of the carriage and mustered a few local worthies to set up a road block. As the carriage passed under a bridge it was forced to a halt and the royal family were identified. They spent a miserable night in the home of the local deputy mayor before returning to their carriage for the long, slow, humiliating journey back to Paris. The illusion of a compromise between the king and his people had finally been shattered.

The story of the royal family's flight is both a cliff-hanger and a comedy of errors. Surrounding it are some of the biggest 'What If's' of the French Revolution. What if the king had not fled but stayed to co-operate with the new Revolutionary government in its efforts to establish a constitutional monarchy? What if the royal family had reached safety and been able to mobilize their allies-in-waiting to return and triumph over their adversaries? If there was a single incident which drove the Revolution into its downward spiral of murderous violence it was the bungled flight to Varennes. Until that moment France had been riding high on a wave of optimism. The hopes generated by 1789 were slowly being translated into a new constitution which seemed to realize the vision of the Enlightenment. The king's flight marked the high watermark of this tide and caused it to turn overnight.

A wave of panic hit France when it became known that the king had tried to flee, followed by a profound sense of betrayal. His ignominious return to Paris was greeted by a silent throng in whom the hatred was palpable. A feeble attempt by the National Assembly to portray the escape as a kidnapping was soon shown to be ridiculous.

The king had left behind a letter declaring his renunciation of the Revolution and its constitution. Later, on the eve of his trial, secret papers were unearthed which showed him and the queen to have been in league with France's enemies. This was treason of the highest magnitude, a stab at the heart of the Revolution by the head of state himself.

From that moment, the messianic hope of a new age evaporated. In its place, fuelled by the discovery of the king's duplicity and the secret machinations of the royal couple, came a pervasive fear of enemy invasion. France was taken over by an atmosphere of paranoia, and with it came a new set of leaders, whose personal paranoia resonated with that of the country.

Foremost amongst these was Robespierre, waiting in the wings for his moment. The prospect of an enemy invasion, which was already looming across the border, had suddenly materialized on France's doorstep in the form of the king himself. There were immediate calls for the deposition of the king and the establishment of a republic. The war which had been threatening broke out in April 1792, and renewed feelings of panic and rage swept the country. Paris became the centre of a new radical brand of revolutionaries led by the Jacobins and more extreme elements who gave vent to murderous feelings against those identified as enemies of the people.

The next stage in the attack on the mythical monster took the form of the demolition of the monarchy. On 10th August 1792 the ringing of the tocsin summoned the people onto the streets to fight against the forces of the counter-revolution. Louis and his family were driven from the palace. In an attempt to avoid further bloodshed, Louis gave the order for his Swiss guard to lay down their arms, at which they were massacred by the armed throng. The young Napoleon, who was among the crowd watching the scene, mused that a whiff of grapeshot would have saved the day for Louis.

The king had been deposed and a republic declared. Now the question of what to do with the royal family arose. Until this could be decided they were taken into captivity in a fortified prison-like building once used in medieval times by the knights Templar. Here Louis conducted himself with quiet dignity, disciplining himself into a routine which included reading, prayer, and the task to which he applied himself most assiduously, the education of his son. With paranoia rampant, his lessons in mathematics had to be abandoned, however, because he was suspected of teaching the little boy to write messages in code.

— ❖ —

In the final act of the scapegoat myth, Louis the man of flesh and blood was made to face trial for the crimes of Louis the tyrant. The arguments which raged at his trial contained no pleas for compassion. The case for the prosecution was, as Robespierre put it, that Louis would have to die so that the republic could live on. According to Robespierre's logic it was not even necessary to try Louis. He stood condemned by his very existence as king. One symbol of sovereignty, the monarch, had to be executed so that another symbol of sovereignty, the republic, could survive. It was a bizarre piece of logic, effectively denying the difference between a person and an abstraction, but it carried the day. On 21st January 1793, Louis travelled in a closed carriage to the guillotine, to the sound of steady drumbeats and in the presence of a silent throng. His anguished family learnt of his death from the sound of a cannon and jubilant shouts of 'Long live the Republic!'

Nine months later, on 16th October 1793, Marie Antoinette followed her husband to the guillotine. Her humiliation continued to the end. There was no closed carriage to provide a shield from the masses along the way. She was forced to make the journey in an open tumbril which had served as a refuse cart. A famous sketch by the revolutionary artist David captures her at that moment, a haggard, expressionless woman, her unkempt, shorn grey hair protruding from her bonnet of the condemned.

Her trial had been stage-managed by two of the Revolution's most rabid figures, Chaumette and Hébert. The latter had waged a long and obscene campaign against the royal family. With the king gone, he devoted himself to an attack on the queen peppered with foul and abusive rhetoric. One of his strategies was to coerce the dauphin to testify against his mother that she had forced him to have sexual intercourse with her. Shaken from her numbness by this allegation, Marie Antoinette rose to make an impassioned appeal to the women in the gallery to support her against this affront to motherhood. Her plea stirred a wave of sympathy which prompted Robespierre, who had no qualms about executing the queen, to censure Hébert and put a stop to that line of questioning.

The destruction of the remaining tentacles of the monster continued apace. On 10th May, 1794, the king's sister, Madame Elisabeth, was taken to the guillotine. The prosecution had decided that as a member of the 'detestable family' she had 'co-operated in all the plots and conspiracies' and that these were 'too well known to make it necessary to repaint the horrible picture'. Ominously, though, there were no cries of 'Vive la Revolution' after her execution, and the watching crowd dispersed silently.

The two royal children still remained as prisoners in the temple. Of these, by far the more dangerous in the fevered minds of the revolutionary leaders was the nine-year-old dauphin, Louis-Charles, who, if the Revolution had not come, would have ascended the throne as Louis XVII, and who still had the potential to become the focus of a royalist resurgence. His custodians could not bring themselves to kill him outright. Instead, they allowed him to languish in appalling conditions, withdrawn into muteness, infested and malnourished, until his death eighteen months after his mother's execution.

The sole survivor of the family in the temple was the dauphin's older sister, Marie Thérèse. A few days after the death of her brother the Convention was suddenly reminded by a delegation petitioning her release that 'the daughter of Louis XVI is languishing within a horrible prison . . . deprived of every comfort and support'. Finally, at the age of sixteen, she was exchanged for French prisoners held by Austria, and returned to a country she had never known.

Nowhere else in story of the Revolution is the mind's difficulty in separating the symbol from the actuality, the group from the real people who comprise that group, more clearly evident than in the revolutionaries' efforts to extirpate the French royal family. The revolutionaries were able to rationalize acts of torture, abuse, humiliation and murder perpetrated against a father, mother and children who were doomed, not for who they were as persons, but for what they represented, to a group heavily traumatized by centuries of oppression – a monstrous, evil family who had to be destroyed to save the Revolution. As the wheel of the Revolution swung round, the victims of tyranny were turning into perpetrators, just as the pigs in George Orwell's *Animal Farm* eventually metamorphosed into the hated humans. It is a story as old as the human condition, carrying the hope, nevertheless, that the cycle could be broken if only it could be understood.

CHAPTER TWO

Robespierre
The Mind of a Fanatic

'If it were not for my conscience, I would be the unhappiest man alive.'
Robespierre, July 1794

These words, written above the text of his last speech but never delivered, encapsulate the essential conflict of the man. Happiness for Robespierre lay in civic duty, which meant the promulgation of the Revolution towards the fulfilment of his dream of the perfect society. Idealism and paranoia lay side by side in his mind, separated only by a thin partition which readily dissolved whenever the dream was threatened by his enemies.

Robespierre held with delusional conviction the belief that he was doing the right thing, but no amount of devotion to duty could compensate him for his sense of isolation. His only friendships were based on his affinity with those who shared his view of the Revolution. He was admired and idolized but he could never give or receive unconditional personal love. He gained his sense of self by fusing his identity with that of the Revolution, a grandiose self-definition which gained him the reputation among those who disagreed with him of being, like Byron, mad, bad and dangerous to know. In his own mind he *was* the Revolution and the survival of the Revolution was inextricably bound up with his own survival.

In appearance he was a pale-complexioned, slightly built, tense figure, dressed to the point of foppishness, wearing the powdered wig and costume of the aristocrats whom he hated. His behavior at the tribune suggested a self-consciousness which betrayed itself in his efforts to appear taller than he was. He had a disconcerting habit of raising his spectacles to his forehead, pausing and slowly looking around him as if to hunt out his enemies before resuming his speech. His voice was harsh and high-pitched, his Breton accent a topic for mockery in the early days of his interminable speech-making. Later it was the content of his speeches which held his audience in thrall.

Occasionally he showed glimmerings of a dry humour and he was not without an altruistic concern for childhood friends provided they posed no political threat. He acted as a confidant to one of the daughters of his landlord and enjoyed the company of her sister in walks with his pet dog along the river bank but there was no suggestion of sexual entanglement with either of these young women. Despite hints of an engagement to a woman during his early years as a lawyer in Arras the affair came to naught and he appeared for the rest of his days to settle into a celibate existence more in keeping with a monastic lifestyle. Robespierre the puritan could not be deflected from his life's work of safeguarding the Revolution for France.

The few friends he had were his political comrades in arms. The price for his friendship was total commitment to his ideology. He kept a protective eye on his former school friend Desmoulins, and was capable of writing a compassionate letter of sympathy to his powerful rival Danton on the death of his first wife. But he never forgot an insult and he made no distinction between the personal and the political in this regard. When Desmoulins went a step too far in challenging Robespierre's conception of the Terror there was only one warning from Robespierre before his impetuous erstwhile friend was dispatched to the guillotine.

His relationship with Danton was complicated by mutual contempt. Danton's flamboyant lifestyle and boisterous manner irritated Robespierre beyond measure. When Robespierre waxed eloquent about his cherished concept of virtue, Danton famously taunted him with the remark that virtue was what he, Danton, did with his wife every night. Robespierre could do nothing in the face of such provocation, but he kept notes, and as time went by he cobbled together Danton's foibles into a case for corruption and betrayal of the Revolution.

Danton's political flirtations with royalty, his tainted association with a general who had defected to the enemy and his involvement in a financial scandal provided all the evidence that Robespierre needed to drive home his argument that Danton had veered away from the principles of the Revolution and 'indulged' his enemies instead of destroying them. But he did not exult in the deaths of his fellow revolutionaries. He had pleaded with Desmoulins to change his ways before striking him down, and he agonized before adding his signature in an uncharacteristically tiny script to the warrant for Danton's execution.

How, then, is it possible to understand the terrifying power wielded by a man so unprepossessing in appearance, uncharismatic in manner and devoid of social charm? It is true that he possessed enormous drive and dedication. The Revolution for him was a matter of life and death. But there are many zealots, religious and secular, who never advance beyond their soapbox.

The key to his success lay in his uncanny ability to articulate the needs of the embittered, oppressed victims of the *ancien regime* and offer them a vision of salvation. In talking for these people he was also talking for himself. Their needs were his needs, their rage was his rage, their vision his. But this can only be part of the explanation. To understand both his success and his failure as a leader we will have to visit his childhood, reconstruct his formative experiences as best we can and try to fathom the workings of his inner world.

When he was six years old his mother died. His father, also a lawyer by training, was a feckless character who left his four children in the care of reluctant relatives after the death of his wife and disappeared soon afterwards from the family's home town of Arras.

By the age of seven, Maximilien had effectively lost both his parents. His father returned to Arras from time to time to cadge money from the family but he never stayed long enough to become a meaningful presence in his children's lives. A paper trail of documents suggests that he wandered through Northern France and Germany in search of work as either a lawyer or a teacher, and that he died in Munich when Maximilien was eighteen years old. As far as Maximilien was concerned, however, his father had died when he walked out on his children.

There is no reliable evidence about the quality of Maximilien's relationship with his parents. He never spoke about them and we have to fall back on his younger sister Charlotte, who hero-worshipped him, to give us the closest picture we have of him through her memoirs written in old age at the behest of one of Robespierre's loyal disciples.

The loss of both his parents at such a tender age would have left a deep emotional scar. His mother had been pregnant with her fifth child. The baby was stillborn and its birth carried away the mother as well. It was the convergence of birth and death which would have shocked and confused Maximilien. A void suddenly opened up in his life which remained unfilled despite the intellectual efforts of his six year old mind. Loss and abandonment would remain the dominant traumas of his life. A child of six still sees himself as the centre of the world. If something terrible happens he blames himself, in much the same way that adults frantically search their minds after an accident to discover thoughts or actions which might have caused it. When tragedy strikes in childhood, the undeveloped mind relies heavily on magical thinking to explain events. One of the great difficulties about adult relationships is that the connections forged in the mind by early trauma and loss do not yield easily to the powers of reason in later life.

Robespierre probably reproached himself for his mother's death. In his mind he may even have been responsible for it, and he would have developed a determination to make good. From then on he would behave impeccably and deny himself the ordinary pleasures and indulgences of life. He would no longer care about himself. His mother's death had given him a mission: To bring her back to life, not in the flesh, but in the creation of a new world, where everyone would get looked after and no one would experience the hurt and pain of loss.

Overnight he became a little adult. He lost his playfulness, disciplined his emotions and brooded incessantly about the best way to achieve his promised land. Charlotte describes him as playing quietly by himself for long periods, seeking comfort by building model chapels, reading, and ministering to his pet pigeons. In one anecdote she chastises herself for having neglected one of the birds which he had hesitantly entrusted to her care. As a result it died, and Charlotte was left with the anguished memory of her brother's silent reproach.

A child's mind simplifies the world into black and white, good and evil, the more so if there has been a catastrophic loss. If Robespierre idealized his mother, the counterpoint would have been the demonization of his vanished father. In her memoirs Charlotte excuses her father's absence from home with the romantic justification that he had been compelled to travel in order to assuage his grief. This may have been one reason for his disappearance from the family's home town of Arras, although it does not explain why he failed to attend his wife's funeral.

Another reason for his travels may have been the fact that he was held in poor esteem by the Arras community, including his fellow lawyers, and that he had been forced to move on in order to find work. He had also probably fallen out with his wife's parents. Just as he had not attended their daughter's funeral, so had they not attended her forced wedding to this dissolute young man with his feeble career prospects. Maximilien almost certainly did not share his sister's charitable interpretation of their father's behaviour. As far as he was he was concerned his father had been derelict in his duties as a father and provider. He was determined to become the very opposite: Responsible not only for his family but for the whole world, a world in which the spirit of his mother was embodied.

Beneath Maximilien's dark dreams and grandiose plans he was profoundly depressed. Charlotte speaks of their childhood as being 'bathed in tears'. She remembers her brother retreating into a corner when they were together and only joining in play with his younger siblings in order to supervise their games. When the children were in their late teens, Henriette, the younger of the two sisters, died, and this added to their sense of inconsolable loss.

Beneath all depression lies a reservoir of anger. It was this anger in Maximilen that would one day rise to the surface and transform itself into a rage and hatred that would make him want to destroy all those who stood in the way of the realization of his dream. His father would multiply into many fathers, all of them corrupt, all of them using their power to attack and kill his beautiful and virtuous mother, symbolized in his republic of virtue. These selfish, malevolent fathers would annihilate the new world being created by the revolution unless they were stopped.

There were many sins for which Maximilien could never forgive his father. The cardinal one was the desertion of his children at their time of greatest emotional need. Another was the fact that his father had selfishly bargained away the children's financial inheritance to gain immediate respite from his debts. This seems to have been the sole purpose of at least one of his father's visits to his relatives in Arras. Any fleeting contact that he might have had with the children during these visits would have done nothing to alleviate the pain of his prolonged absences. On the contrary, it would only have heightened their sense of loss and fuelled the anger which underlay it. Their father's disposal of the family silver, leaving his children edging towards poverty, would have seemed like the final act of betrayal, a destruction of trust which haunted Robespierre in all his adult relationships.

Another of his father's sins was to rankle in the recesses of Maximilien's mind. He had had a narrow escape from the stigma of illegitimacy. His parents' marriage on 2nd January 1758 was followed only four months later, on 6th May, by Maximilien's birth. Their hasty marriage had averted the legal stigma, but tongues would still wag. Arras was the provincial capital of Artois, a town brimming with clerics and lawyers, and there would have been plenty of townsfolk, cloaked in the garb of religious respectability, to cluck and gossip about the scandalous behaviour of Maximilien de Robespierre senior. Little Maximilien would have felt the shame of this, and it would have intensified his simmering rage. Later he would write an essay on the responsibilities of the state in the protection of the rights of illegitimate children.

Maximilien's mother, Jacqueline Carraut, was the daughter of a well-to-do brewer, while the de Robespierres, despite the pretentious nobiliary particle which flapped from their surname and the title of barrister which attached to both Maximilien's father and his paternal grandfather, were a family in decline. An obvious inference was that his father had seduced his mother in the hope of improving his precarious social and economic status. The resentment of Jacqueline's parents towards their son-in-law for impregnating their daughter and forcing the marriage was another emotional bequest from his father to Maximilien. His maternal grandparents, saddled with the responsibility and part care of the de Robespierre children, would have been unlikely to disguise their feelings towards the children's father.

Robespierre's self-imposed burden of responsibility would have been reinforced by the emotional reactions of his three younger siblings to their mother's death. They turned towards him as one, attached themselves to him with all the intensity of anxious, grieving children and converted him into their new parent. For the rest of his life he remained *in loco parentis*, a stern, wise father figure who dispensed judgment, advice and practical support and arbitrated in their quarrels. In return, they gave him their undying loyalty. Being in charge of his hero-worshipping sisters and brother was a role that suited him well. He had a precocious solemnity, and the clinging dependence of his siblings gave him a sense of power and self-importance. The mask of quiet authority was needed to hide his own emotional turmoil. From now on he would be the head of the family, the commander of their rudderless ship as it rose and fell on the waves.

Charlotte's rose-tinted memoirs stand in contrast to the jaundiced recollections of others who knew him as a child. The future revolutionary Stanislas Fréron, who was at school with him at Louis-le-Grand College, and who of course was not going to taint himself with any fond reminiscences of the late tyrant, remembers him with a long list of unflattering adjectives. For Fréron he was, amongst other things, secretive, morose, vindictive, jealous, unforgiving and dishonest. Yet the two profiles, Charlotte's idealized portrait and Fréron's portrayal of him as an embryonic tyrant, are strangely congruent. In both the young Robespierre emerges as remote, reserved and austere, a dreamer, a child with a melancholy disposition and an anger that lay just below the surface. But while Charlotte saw his aloofness as sadness, his reserve as kind and gentle, his anger as an emotion in the service of the underdog harnessed to protect other children from being bullied, Fréron construed those same features as dangerous and imparted to them the cold-blooded menace of a crocodile lying in wait for victims beneath the surface of the water.

Charlotte lived her own life in the shadow of her older brother. In exchange for his fatherly protection she looked after him in adult life with nun-like devotion, fussing over him like an anxious mother and defending him indignantly against his critics. Her aunts had dispatched her to a convent boarding school at the age of eight, where she was groomed for the life of a submissive, self-sacrificing woman. She basked in his glory, kept house for him when he stayed in Arras, and she followed him to Paris after his election to the National Convention.

In Paris she was dismayed to find that he was already being pampered and hero-worshipped by a family of Jacobins, the Duplays, who had adopted him. A short illness of Maximilien gave Charlotte the chance to enter into a tug of love with Mme Duplay, which she lost. Despite her resentment towards Maximilien because of this, her loyalty towards him remained undimmed. Charlotte outlived her brother by forty years. After his execution she was imprisoned and subjected to humiliation and abuse. Embittered, she went on to lead a reclusive life, living off a pension granted to her by Napoleon, who had been a friend of their brother Augustin and who held a sympathetic view of Maximilien. Napoleon contended that Robespierre's main failing lay in his ignorance of military matters.

Augustin was a different kettle of fish. His pet name, *bonbon,* gives a flavour of his more engaging and outgoing disposition. Like his older sisters, he idolized Maximilien and looked to him as a source of paternal authority and wise counsel. He followed Maximilien closely along his career path, inheriting his scholarship at the prestigious Louis-le-Grand College, studying law and becoming a deputy in the National Convention, where he pursued the same brand of revolutionary politics as his brother. But he was altogether a more visceral character than Maximilien, robust in his relationships with women and not averse to joining battle as a soldier in the war against the counter-revolution. In the dramatic moments of his brother's arrest on 9th Thermidor he made a self-sacrificial gesture of brotherly love by demanding that he too be arrested. The two brothers lay together in the tumbril which took them to the guillotine.

One vignette survives of Robespierre and his mother together. Against a background of domestic bliss, once again conveyed by Charlotte, we see little Maximilien being taught the art of lace-making at his mother's knee. The contrast between his apparently secure attachment to his mother before her death and the frightening abyss which opened up for him afterwards offers a plausible explanation for his later moods. To have been loved and nurtured in safety, and then to have had the source of this love torn from him overnight would have been a certain prescription for the anger and fear which ravaged his adult thinking.

There is nothing to suggest that his early years were blighted by brutality or abuse. This has to be acknowledged when trying to understand the mind of a man who stands in the dock of history charged with crimes against humanity. The pattern of the abused child turned abuser is well recognized in history as in everyday life. But this is not a profile which sits comfortably with Robespierre. He was neither a sadist nor bully. The evidence is to the contrary, that he sprang to the defence of schoolmates who were being bullied, and that from his earliest years he harboured a strong identification with the underdogs and victims of society. As a lawyer and judge he had flinched from pronouncing the death sentence, and he had made a passionate plea for its abolition early in his revolutionary career. Throughout the Terror he recoiled from the spectacle of the guillotine, even though his signature had consigned many to it.

Robespierre's childhood ended with the death of his mother. What he was left with was an overwhelming sense of anger and responsibility. Anger is like a highly reactive chemical that cannot exist in isolation. It must combine with a target, whether that turns out to be a particular person, group or symbolic abstraction. Robespierre's anger was primarily directed at himself, causing depression, or as he put it, 'unhappiness'.

His absent father would become an object of murderous rage for not having being there to protect him from the vicissitudes of life. His mother, too, would be a target for his anger, for dying on him. But the thought of harbouring anger toward his mother was unbearable. He would have to preserve her as a good person, and more than that, a goddess, whose memory he could worship and whose example he could follow. The corollary of this would have been an even more intense hatred of his father. The split which was to destroy him in his adulthood was in already in place at the age of seven.

Anger is also an irritant to the mind. If it is held in, unable to escape and react with its external targets, it causes pain. To escape this pain Robespierre hurled his anger outwards, like thunderbolts. In psychological terms, he projected his anger at those who came to represent hated aspects of himself and his father. . Having disowned these parts of himself and lodged them elsewhere he could watch them from a safe distance and control them. So much was projected into the heroes and demons of the outer world that his inner self was depleted. His world was peopled with agents of good and evil who were partly real and partly fantastical. To a large extent they were part of him, but he could not distinguish between his inner self and the 'other'. The battle which raged within him became displaced onto the battlefield out there.

The Revolution gave him the political power he needed in order to realize his fantasies. Despite his iron self-control the seeds of violence lay within him, waiting to sprout in the fertile soil of revolutionary discontent. The dreams of a better society and an end to tyranny with liberty and equality for all were dreams which he shared with many others as the wave of the Enlightenment rolled over Europe. He worked feverishly to bring them to fruition. When opposition to them reared its head he fought ferociously to attack it. His fanatical dedication to the revolutionary cause lay in the fact that he was not just fighting for the survival of his vision, he was fighting for his own survival. His inner self and his vision of a better world had merged. If violence was needed to protect this vision, so be it. He would shut out of his mind any thought of the bloody consequences of such a fight and turn it into a matter of life and death.

While Robespierre's emotional life atrophied, his intellectual life blossomed. Catholic France had entrusted the education of its children to the Oratorians, a more enlightened order than the Jesuits, whose educational mission had been confiscated by Louis XV in 1764. It was priests from this order who nurtured Maximilien's mind, first in Arras and then in Paris.

The introverted little boy who had retired from childhood at the age of six to nurse his dreams discovered a talent in himself which promised compensation for his bleak existence. He was a good reader. His grandparents noticed this, and in any case they wanted him to have an education which would equip him for survival within the ranks of the professional class into which he had been born. They sent him to the College of St Vaast in Arras, a school run by Oratorians who were not slow in spotting the intelligence and diligence in their new pupil. They saw in little Maximilien a future bearer of the Catholic flame of learning, and encouraged him in his studies.

Perhaps for the first time in his life since his mother's death Robespierre experienced admiration, and it warmed his heart. He threw himself into his studies with an intensity which pleased his teachers. Here was a child with a voracious appetite for learning and a devotion to study which could not be shaken by childish pranks or temptations. And he could do more than absorb. He could spout classical prose and poetry with a precocious earnestness which earned him plaudits in the classroom and sent him up to the platform to recite at special gatherings to celebrate important occasions.

Maximilien's studiousness and his aptitude for language and ideas brought him to the attention of the Abbe of St Vaast Cathedral. This august cleric had connections with the prestigious College of Louis-le-Grand in Paris and put Robespierre's name forward for a scholarship. Soon afterwards he was saying a tearful farewell to his family and rattling off in a coach on the hundred or so mile trip to Paris. For the rest of his life Arras and Paris would be the two geographic poles of his existence. His horizons would never expand beyond France, and he seldom left Paris. In his vast blueprint for a better world, external space did not matter to him. Paris was simply an annex to his room in Arras, where he could work on putting his schemes into action.

In the meantime, his education would continue at the finest school in France. Louis-le-Grand College had been founded in 1379 and was, in its own way, an enlightened establishment. The Oratorians who had taken over from the Jesuits still ran a tight ship. Prayer and study filled the child's day from dawn till dusk, and there was no chance to sneak out and go adventuring in the alluringly sordid streets of the left bank of the Seine, which lay a stone's throw outside the walls. But there was no draconian discipline. Corporal punishment had been discarded and the teachers implemented a policy of benign encouragement towards open-mindedness within the constraints of an education governed by a holy order. There was every opportunity for the pupils to dip into the literature which was coming out of the Enlightenment and to smuggle in racy novels such as Rousseau's *Emile*, the story of a priest who falls in love with a young woman and abandons the priesthood.

In this facilitating setting Robespierre's impressionable mind opened up to the fresh streams of thought which now flowed into it. His world had suddenly grown larger. The earliest circuits of his mind, his family matrix, had been laid down during his childhood in Arras. He already knew with certainty that parents could not be trusted, that children had to look after themselves, and that relatives would provide bread and butter but not love. Now he was about to discover this second matrix, a much larger network peopled by fellow scholars and teachers, and beyond them by a world of thinkers whom he could only meet through the printed word.

Beyond these again were many others long dead, the heroes of past ages, their memories kept alive through the legends and classical writings placed at his disposal in the classrooms and library of Louis-le-Grand. This new social matrix would embed itself in his mind and resonate with his family matrix. The tyrants of history would fill the space vacated by his absent father, whose departure had let them in. For the first time Robespierre could identify with real people, the heroes of antiquity, Greeks, Romans and Spartans who had fought and defeated these tyrants and set up states where justice and freedom prevailed. The hazy dream of a paradise where he could be re-united with his mother could now assume the more clearly defined shape of a land in which good behaviour would be rewarded, where everyone could have a voice and rule together. He was beginning to sculpt his republic of virtue out of this ancient clay.

There was further nourishment to be had from the writings of the living prophets of an enlightened age. One of these was a slightly built man with spindly legs – one historian described him as a brain on sticks. François-Marie Arouet, who wrote under the name of Voltaire, was a prolific writer of satire, poetry and polemics. His outraged assaults on the injustice and barbarism of the regime had already earned him exile and a spell of imprisonment in the Bastille, and his acidic writings on blind optimism and unquestioning faith, recorded most famously in his picaresque novel *Candide*, had already etched themselves deeply into the society of his day.

When Robespierre arrived at Louis-le-Grand in 1764 Voltaire was already approaching seventy. His personal suffering, his crusade against injustice and his view that reason and belief in a supreme being could exist side by side would have found a perfect resonance with the young Robespierre's burgeoning world view.

The most influential figure in Robespierre's life was Jean Jacques Rousseau. Robespierre idealized Rousseau and identified with him in a fashion that transcended mere intellectual affinity. There was a curious parallel in their earliest years: Rousseau's mother had died within days of giving birth to him and his father had abandoned him when he was ten, giving him over into the care of an uncle, who passed him on to the local village school, where he was indoctrinated in Calvinism. Rousseau's picaresque journeys and his sexual adventures, however, bore no resemblance to Robespierre's one-track path through life, but the persecution suffered by Rousseau and the identity of their political and philosophical visions would have been enough to seal Robespierre's bond. He wrote ecstatically about a pilgrimage which he had made to Rousseau's home on the outskirts of Paris when he was fifteen years old, when he had caught sight of the old man reposing in his garden. It was the classic case of an enduring adolescent infatuation. *The Social Contract* was Robespierre's bible. He kept a copy of it by his bedside.

Robespierre's was a mind in torment, a mind split by the contradictory need to destroy the old world and build a new one, to relieve suffering in some while inflicting it on others. It was a paradox which no amount of reasoning or logic could resolve. In childhood it had been simple. He could place his enemies in one compartment of his mind, safely locked away until a means could be found for their disposal, and he could concentrate his energies on the elaboration of his dream. As the conflict which was the Revolution deepened, he came increasingly into conflict with himself. The childhood solution which had seemed so neat was no longer holding. Towards the end of his young life the enemies in his mind would intrude increasingly into the other compartment, reserved for friends and allies of the Revolution. The partitions between the two compartments would break down. And his mind would crack.

Throughout his life Robespierre tried desperately to reconcile these contradictions with his powers of reasoning and intellect. When these failed he did what he had done as a child: He retreated into a corner and nursed himself back to equanimity in solitude. The problem, however, was that although he could re-design his inner mental architecture to prove yet again that he was right, there were progressively fewer people out there in the real world who would agree with him. When he rejoined the world of the 'other' his solitude stayed with him and isolated him from his confederates.

Where was the 'good' in this epic battle? The two features of the human mind which elevate it above the rest of the animal kingdom are its intellect and its capacity to empathize with others. Intellect gives us our capacity for rendering feelings into thoughts and forging them into ideas, concepts and formulations which can be built into systems and translated into social action. Empathy gives us our ability to understand the thoughts and feelings of our fellow human beings as if they were our own, to welcome affinities and respect differences. Robespierre was well endowed intellectually but he suffered from an empathic blindness. He could fall in love with an idea but not a person. It can be said of him – and many like him – that he loved mankind but hated men.

Robespierre was undoubtedly paranoid, in the sense of someone whose view of the world is almost entirely self-referent. When things are going well, the paranoid individual assumes a grandiose responsibility for what is happening. Conversely, when things are going badly, the same individual feels persecuted and attacked. There is no middle ground or sense of shared responsibility. Robespierre's grandiosity came into full flood when the tide of the Revolution reached its high watermark, with the overthrow of the monarchy and the defeat of

France's external enemies. The persecutory side of his paranoia came to the fore when the violence of the Revolution ran out of control. This side of him was rooted in his childhood experience that the people on whom he had relied could not be trusted. The obverse of trust was betrayal. Parents tended to betray you by abandoning you when you most needed them, leaving you to the mercy of those who considered themselves superior to you for no reason other than an accident of birth. The remedy was simple. First, these people had to be identified. But because they were also cunning, they resorted to deceit, disguise and hypocrisy. Unless you were clever enough to unmask them they would destroy you before you could destroy them, together with everything you held precious.

Robespierre transferred this simplistic world view, the blueprint of which lay in his childhood, onto the larger political canvas of France. He ascended laboriously to the pinnacle of his power in order to apply his remedy for curing the evils of society, but it was power without muscle, the ambiguous power of rhetoric and the fickle power of the law, both of which were turned against him when his enemies of different colours united out of fear in order to bring him down.

CHAPTER THREE

Danton
The Passionate Opportunist

*'I'm leaving everything in a frightful mess. There's not a single one of
them who knows the first thing about government . . . If I left my
balls to that eunuch Robespierre and my legs to Couthon the
Committee of Public Safety might last a bit longer. But . . . as
it is Robespierre is bound to follow me, dragged down by
me. Ah, better to be a poor fisherman than muck
about with politics.'*
Danton (awaiting his execution)

Throughout his life Georges Jacques Danton threw himself at the
world with a recklessness which brought him grief and reward in equal
measure. Unlike the fastidious Robespierre he exulted in physical
pleasure and the fray of battle. As a boy on his grandfather's farm in
rural Champagne he had several encounters with farm animals which
resulted in facial injuries and lifelong disfigurement – a torn lip and
broken nose inflicted by an angry bull, and scars on his cheeks and
eyelids, the result of being trampled on by a herd of pigs. Added to
this were the ravages of smallpox. To his enemies the ugliness of his
features and the coarseness of his language mirrored the brutishness
of his nature. Yet his earthy warmth was attractive to women and he
proved to be a devoted husband and father and a staunch friend. He
was a person for whom ties of affection and personal regard mattered
more than political or religious principles.

Danton's grandparents were peasant farmers who had worked hard
to improve their lot. His father had left that world behind to become
a legal clerk, thereby lifting the family into a comfortable middle-class
existence without severing their bond to the countryside. Georges was
born in Arcis, a small town in the Champagne district, some hundred
miles to the south-east of Paris, close to the tranquil river Aube and
edged by farmland. He formed a sentimental attachment to this town
and the bucolic lifestyle which surrounded it. Time and again he
returned there to gain respite from the turbulence and madness of the

Revolution. It was in Arcis that he could regenerate himself through the love of his family and the cultivation of his plot of land.

Danton's attachment to his home town and his idealization of the countryside played an important part in the shaping of his personality. He was not quite three years old when his father died, leaving his pregnant mother to look after him and his three older sisters. The new baby was stillborn, adding to the family's grief. But Danton's mother was made of sturdy stuff. With the help of her relatives and members of the Arcis community she managed her affairs sensibly and kept up her flow of love for the children. She and her son remained on affectionate terms into her old age. Unlike Robespierre, who had to construct an image of his mother based on a few fragile memories before the age of six, Danton had a lifelong relationship of flesh and blood with a mother who, like her son, met life head on with a mixture of canniness and determination.

There was love in his childhood, but no discipline. Between the ages of three and ten Georges was allowed to run wild. After his father's death life at home became chaotic, with Mme Danton having to cope with a family of noisy children which included the children of her husband's first marriage. She placed her little boy in the hands of a governess, who also failed to control his unruly behaviour. As a young man Danton enjoyed regaling his friends with boastful reminiscences of his childhood exploits. The picture we have is of a free and unbounded childhood. We see him discharging his energy by racing through meadows, fishing, playing with farm lads and swimming in the river Aube. Later, while living in Paris, the young daredevil swam in the Seine, as a result of which he contracted typhoid. The romantic image is always tempered by the reminder that nature can be dangerous. Danton, the impetuous, risk-taking child was also an angry child, asking to be firmly held and protected from the vicissitudes of nature.

He had reason enough to be angry. His father had died at the moment in his development when a boy needs his father to be present as an authority figure, loving but strong enough to withstand the child's anger at having to submit to rules and share his mother's love with another person. The story of Oedipus, which Freud regarded as a universal script written into the human mind, predicts tragedy if the son prevails over the father in the struggle to possess the mother. The epic fight between father and son is conducted in the child's unconscious mind and only runs to a happy outcome if the father survives the child's angry onslaught and holds back from his own murderous counter-attack. In Danton's case a terrible reality superimposed itself on the fantasy, in the form of his father's actual death. With all the self-centredness of a three year old, Georges would have concluded that he was responsible for his father's death.

The combination of his father's death and his mother's inability to contain him brought him to the belief that there was no authority in the world other than his own. The rest of his life would be devoted to a blind search for a power strong enough to contain his destructive violence and keep at bay the fear which lay behind it. A child given so much freedom becomes terrified of his own power. With no adult to offer resistance or set limits, the child either turns in on himself and constructs a complicated set of rules by which to lead his life – this was Robespierre's solution – or dashes himself repeatedly against the environment, unconsciously longing to be defeated and seeking the resistance which no one will offer him. Eventually he comes to believe that he is invincible. This was the path chosen by Danton.

When Danton was ten his mother married a local merchant, a widower with a child of his own. This man appears to have been a good-natured husband and stepfather but a hopeless businessman who brought the family to the brink of ruin. He poured money into a scatterbrained project for marketing a device for spinning cotton which went awry, and it was partly through young Danton's intelligent interventions that the family finances were rescued.

At school Danton showed a gift for languages but a stubborn disregard for all other subjects. His aptitudes pointed him the direction of the priesthood and he was packed off to a seminary at nearby Troyes, but he took an instant dislike to the religious atmosphere of the place and implored his stepfather to remove him. The kind man obliged, placing him in lodgings from where he could still continue to attend classes without having to submit to the rigours by which children were groomed for the priesthood. Given this freedom, Danton blossomed into a good all-round scholar.

Danton believed from an early age that his eloquence could open any doors. His friends recalled one episode at school in which he sprang to the defence of a classmate threatened with corporal punishment. The sixteen-year-old Danton, already possessed of the loud, resonant voice that would later thrill the revolutionary crowds, delivered a passionate denunciation of corporal punishment, not only in schools but in the wider society. Incredibly, the rector of the school intervened on Danton's side and forbade the teacher to inflict the punishment. This daring display of advocacy won him widespread admiration and boosted his sense of omnipotence.

Everything about Danton's persona marked him out as a demagogue. He cut an impressive figure, with his giant stature and leonine features, the scarred lips pulled into an expression somewhere between a snarl and a sneer. He used rhetoric like a virtuoso, playing on the mood of his audience. When he raged against his enemies his audience raged with him, when he mocked them his audience applauded him with derisive laughter. His language was full of hyperbole and invective. Captured in print it made him seem like a monster foaming at the mouth, but it was the music that mattered more than the content, which seemed to evaporate afterwards. His booming voice reminded people of Mirabeau, the great orator of the States General, whom he resembled in appearance as well as in declamatory style, and whose proclivity for shady dealings on both sides of the revolutionary divide he shared. To the Royalists he was 'the Mirabeau of the mob', a dangerous agitator whose exhortations had contributed to the slaughter of innocents.

In private exchanges he delivered punches and jabs which stayed in the memory. When he heard that Vadier, a radical Jacobin on the Committee of General Security, had referred to him as 'that fat, stuffed turbot' and promised to 'gut' him, he riposted that he would become 'more cruel than a cannibal' and that he would eat the man's brains and shit in his skull. This was the sort of scabrous language in which he was completely at home. The difference was, that, unlike the unsavoury characters with whom he traded insults, he had no intention of translating his words into actions. During the Terror his political energies went into saving lives, not taking them. Like the sorcerer's apprentice he tried to put a stop to the flood of violence which he and many others had released with their rhetoric.

To those who had known him before the Revolution, there was another side to him. They remembered him as a warm, fun-loving person capable of listening as well as talking, a man whose appetite for the visceral pleasures of life was balanced by his wide intellectual interests. As a young lawyer in Paris he radiated a natural sociability which won him friends from all walks of life. He joined a Masonic Lodge, where he rubbed shoulders with distinguished lawyers, aristocrats and future revolutionary luminaries including Mirabeau and the Abbe Sieyès, author of a seminal pamphlet on the Third Estate. When it came to the promoting his career he had no scruples about slipping off to Reims to take a short-cut route to qualification as a barrister instead of submitting to the long and arduous course of study which would have been required of him in Paris. And in the days when official positions were bought he managed to procure the large sum of money required to become an advocate of the King's Council by prevailing on friends, relatives and his future father-in-law to advance him the necessary funds. The charmer and the wheeler dealer were as much part of his make-up as the thrilling orator.

Danton did not have to work too hard to win the heart of the young woman whom he intended to marry. Gabrielle Charpentier was the daughter of an innkeeper in whose premises Danton spent long hours of convivial conversation while Gabrielle, a modest and demure young woman, served the tables. Danton went to great lengths to make a good impression on the family, helped by the fact that he could charm Gabrielle's Italian mother by chatting to her in her native tongue and that her shrewd father saw his daughter's marriage to this ambitious young lawyer as a step up the social ladder. Danton worked his magic on Gabrielle too, displacing a rival suitor along the way. The wedding was a grand occasion with a dinner and ball for about a hundred guests including Danton's sixty-seven year old mother and his many relatives from the sticks.

Danton's life after his marriage to Gabrielle is the familiar story of a man caught between the allure of politics and the love of his family. As the factional rivalries intensified, such divided loyalties became a matter of life and death. Events were moving too fast for a political leader of Danton's stature to afford the indulgence of prolonged absences from the political arena. By 1792 assemblies and committees were meeting night and day to try and keep control of the Revolution, and Danton's devil-may-care attitude to the tedium of meetings, report writing and accurate account-keeping presented his enemies with heaven-sent opportunities for bringing him down. He seemed to think that it would be enough for him to materialize from time to time, mount the podium and exercise his rhetoric to swing the arguments his way. The love of his wife and family provided him with a good reason to spend time at home, but he was also overtaken by periodic bouts of indolence suggestive of depression, which drove him into retreat. During these moods he voiced pessimism about the future of the Revolution and railed against the stupidity of his fellow politicians,

In February 1793 Gabrielle died while giving birth to their third child. Danton poured out his grief with the same explosive passion with which he vented all his other emotions, but he forced himself back into the political fray and within a few months had married again. His second wife, Louise Gély, was barely sixteen years old. She had already been part of the Danton household as Gabrielle's trusted friend and helpmate, and it seems as if Gabrielle had asked her to take on the care of the children in the event of her death. The families on all sides accepted that marriage between Danton and Louise was a better solution to the needs of the children than the possibility of an unknown stepmother coming onto the scene. Danton's affections transferred easily to his new bride, who despite her youthfulness and demure appearance exercised tighter control over him than the innocent

Gabrielle, who had suffered throughout their marriage in the knowledge of her husband's compulsive womanising. The couple were secretly married by a non-conforming priest at the insistence of Louise's father, a Catholic with royalist sympathies. None of this troubled Danton in the slightest. As always, his private life and loves took precedence over the revolutionary ideas to which he paid lip service.

Every political leader has his moment of greatness, the high watermark of his career when his vision, talents and personal attributes run together and harmonize with the needs of the people. Danton's moment came in September 1792 when the French army was being pushed back by the Prussians. The defence of two key fortresses, Longwy and Verdun, had collapsed and the way was open to an attack on Paris. In the ensuing panic Danton was the only member of the revolutionary government to keep his head. He rebuked his fellow ministers for their defeatism and quashed their proposal to evacuate Paris and pull the king out of reach of the enemy. With demonic energy he drummed up arms for the defence of the city and galvanized the citizens of Paris into battle mode.

On the day after the news that Verdun had fallen, he addressed the Legislative Assembly. With a fine touch of the theatrical he entered the assembly hall dressed in an eye-catching scarlet coat, accompanied by his wife. The opening cadences of his speech sounded a note of paradoxical assurance: 'It is a satisfying duty, gentlemen, for the ministers of a free people to have to inform them that their country is going to be saved. The nation is roused and ready for action, impatient to join battle . . . ' Then, in a crescendo of emotion he roared out the promise of victory and the threat of death to those who refused the call to arms. It was a stunning performance which ended with the phrase which was to be reverently quoted by his admirers: 'Boldness, boldness at all times, and yet more boldness, and France will be saved!' *(Pour les vaincre, Messieurs, il nous faut de l'audace, encore de l'audace, toujours de l'audace et la France est sauvée!)*

Intuitively, Danton had found the right language to unify the people. We can see in him the Churchillian art of starting on a sombre note, then building up to a dramatic climax which infused people with the belief that they would prevail whatever the cost. Danton's speeches, however, not only roused the people against the external enemy, they had the effect of intensifying the hunt for enemies inside France. The furies which Danton unleashed rushed inwards as well as outwards. With tension, panic and paranoia at an all-time high there was no controlling the anger which spewed out in all directions and engulfed many innocent people. Robespierre was the chief instigator of the campaign against the internal enemy, but there is no doubt that Danton's diatribes help to create the climate in which this campaign could be conducted.

The massacre of some fourteen hundred prisoners being held in Paris gaols which followed the news of the fall of Longwy was one of the bloodiest atrocities of the Revolution. Danton's role in this event has blighted has reputation more than any other episode in his career. He has been held responsible for inciting the killings with his inflammatory rhetoric and then, as Minister of Justice, doing nothing to stop them. The butchery was carried out by gangs of thugs, some of whom set themselves up as makeshift tribunals to impart a sense of justice to the proceedings. As it turned out, more than half of those done to death were being held for offences unrelated to politics. The killing frenzy burnt itself out after three days, but the lowered threshold of violence and the heightened fear which followed it set the stage for the Reign of Terror which was to come. Danton furiously rebutted accusations that he had been in any way responsible for what had happened. But his bombastic statements while the slaughter was going on did nothing to redeem him. 'I don't give a fuck for the prisoners', he is quoted as saying. 'They'll have to take their chances . . . The people are aroused. They're determined to take the law into their own hands.'

Behind the scenes a different side of him showed itself. With a combination of adroit political manoeuvring and subterfuge he managed to rescue several of his friends and colleagues from the clutches of the popular tribunals, the Committee of Public Safety and the Commune. As was so often the case there was a discrepancy between the aggression of his public utterances and the compassion of his actions behind the scenes. His anger pulled him one way, his sympathy another. One example illustrates this: it took no more than a plea to him from an attractive young woman for him to free her aristocratic husband from a prison outside Paris where another massacre was threatened. Robespierre, with his paranoid vigilance and lack of empathy, could only construe Danton's behaviour in abstract terms, as dangerously anti-revolutionary and therefore criminal.

Between the outbreak of the war in April 1792 and the fall of Robespierre in July 1794 the mood in Paris was unremittingly tense and fearful. The leaders of the various factions fought for power in an atmosphere poisoned by threats, denunciations and self-righteous protestations. They had to act quickly and proclaim their revolutionary credentials loudly if they hoped to stay alive in what was becoming a culture of 'kill or be killed'. No one dared to name the basic flaw in revolutionary logic responsible for this rampant paranoia, namely the assumption that the people could only be led by one group. This precluded a pluralistic solution to any conflict and the corresponding acceptance of different political parties, each with a legitimate claim to representation.

When a group which adheres to the myth of unity begins to fragment, tension rises and elements within the group break away or are driven out as scapegoats. The large group of revolutionaries who had formed such a magnificent entity in 1789 became progressively smaller as, one after another, different political factions were identified as deviant to the cause, isolated and driven out or destroyed. The procession of scapegoats was led by the constitutional monarchists, who had the ground cut from under them by the king's flight. War, civil war, continuing economic hardship and religious strife produced fresh splits in the revolutionary movement, and with every split a new conflict arose, which could only be resolved by the isolation and destruction of one of the conflicting parties, who then became the next scapegoats.

Given the criminal connotations of the terms 'party' and 'faction', a terminology was nevertheless needed to describe the different political groupings which survived the fall of the monarchy. The future 'Left' and 'Right' wings of world politics came into being at this point, through a quirk of seating arrangements in the Legislative Assembly. The more radical deputies, dubbed 'men of the mountain', or Montagnards, because they occupied the highest tiers of benches, sat to the left of the president's chair. Their bitter rivals, a loose constellation of more conservative deputies, sat on benches to the right of the president and were known as Girondins, after the Gironde area in the Bordeaux region, where many of them came from. This group had been damaged by its support for a constitutional monarchy and its opposition to the violence and terror perpetrated by the Paris Commune with the backing of Marat and Robespierre. The position of the Girondins was principled but foolish, given the fact that the legislature was in the heart of Paris and therefore at the mercy of the mob. In June 1793 an armed crowd invaded the Assembly and intimidated it into purging itself of the leading Girondins, who promptly became the next batch of scapegoats. True to the dynamic of a group which nominates scapegoats, the surviving deputies breathed a huge sigh of relief, shrugged their shoulders and looked the other way.

Danton's role in this assault, which signalled the end of parliamentary inviolability, was typically ambiguous. He had built his entire political career on the art of running with the hare and hunting with the hounds. Having first tried to woo the Girondins by offering himself as a diplomat in the service of compromise between Right and Left, and having been stung by their rebuff, he now threw himself angrily into the arms of the Montagnards and launched a vitriolic attack on the Girondins. In the months that followed the polarization between the advocates of terror and moderation stretched him to breaking point. He could not disguise the fact that his true nature inclined him towards moderation, and that was enough to mark him out as an enemy in the eyes of the faction who, with the disappearance of the Girondins, were now becoming known as the Robespierrists.

The conflict was evidently too much for him and provoked another of his nervous collapses, expressed through his escape from Paris and retreat to his home town, where he nursed himself back to health by occupying himself with everything but politics. When a neighbour gave him the news that the Girondins had been executed, thinking that he would be pleased, Danton shocked the poor man by berating him for his stupidity. Did he not realize, railed Danton, that this was bad news, that everyone was factious and deserved death as much as the Girondins, and that they would all suffer the same fate?

After the downfall of the Girondins the fight for power became a three-cornered struggle between those who wanted to bring the Terror to an end, those who wanted to pursue it ruthlessly, and those who were wavering between the two extremes. Robespierre was among the waverers, but his mind could not consciously recognize either his own inner conflict or the need for compromise. The only resolution he could envisage was the elimination of his political adversaries on both the Left and the Right. But which way to turn? He rounded first on the Hébertists, the faction which was outflanking him on the Left with its strident calls for an increase in direct representation by the people of the streets and an escalation of the Terror. This faction posed the more immediate threat because of its influence with the *sans-culottes* and the Paris Commune.

The leader of this faction, Jacques Hébert, was one of the Revolution's more unsavoury characters. His newspaper, *Le Père Duchesne,* specialized in obscene attacks on the royal family and calls for the blood of aristocrats and clergy. His militant atheism and unbridled attacks on Christianity got up the nose of Robespierre, who in the midst of the Terror had picked up on an old revolutionary theme of religious tolerance and was nursing into existence his own theistic cult based on the idea of a Supreme Being. From his power base in the

National Convention it was a simple matter for him to denounce Hèbert's atheism as counter-revolutionary and despatch him and his followers to the guillotine. It was then the turn of the moderates, of whom Danton was the undisputed leader.

In the midst of all of the backstabbing Danton behaved like a tired old pugilist trying to stage a comeback without knowing from which direction the next blow was coming. At heart he was a crowd pleaser who revelled in the limelight and only wanted the good life. When he did operate in the shadows it was either to broker peace between warring parties or to rescue people from the violence of the Revolution. He was never interested in destroying his enemies or pursuing murder as a policy.

As the violence of the Revolution spiralled out of control Danton's tactics of bluff and bluster, which had once served him so well, proved to be his undoing. Moreover there was an innocence about him which prevented him from seeing the glint of evil in the eyes of his adversaries until it was too late. Although it was clear after the fall of the Girondins and the Hèbertists that a showdown was inevitable between the two remaining factions, Danton held on to a touching belief that there could be a reconciliation between himself and Robespierre. As a result, he missed his moment. The National Convention had become an arena where speeches were lethal weapons. Danton failed to realize that victory would fall to whoever denounced the other first. He was on his way to address the Convention when he caught sight of Robespierre in the lobby, engaged in what appeared to be a friendly conversation with Desmoulins, a man whose life also hung by a thread after he had antagonized Robespierre with accusations of revolutionary heresy. This amicable scene was enough to reassure Danton that there was no urgent need for him to make his move. He turned on his heel and went home. Meanwhile, the Robespierrists on the Committee of Public Safety, aware of Danton's power to sway audiences, connived to have him arrested before denouncing him to the Convention. He was arrested in the early hours of the morning of 31st March, 1794.

Danton did not go quietly to his death. He may well have had the thought that he would emerge triumphant, just as Marat had done after the Girondins' ill-judged move to bring him before the revolutionary tribunal in 1792. Perhaps he thought that all that was needed for justice to prevail was another display of his old oratorical magic backed up by his mastery of legal procedure. But the puny men who surrounded this giant were under instructions to secure a conviction at all costs. Danton was not tried on his own but as part of a group, a ploy which would taint him by association with those implicated in a financial scandal. Undaunted, Danton dominated the court with demands for witnesses and kept up a withering denunciation of the legality of the proceedings. When he appeared to be winning public sympathy, the increasingly uncomfortable public prosecutor sought advice from his masters on the Committee of Public Safety, pre-eminently Robespierre and St Just who knew that Danton's survival would mean their own death. Between them they found a way of silencing him on the incredible grounds that his arguments had shown him to be in revolt against the authority of the court. Danton and his co-defendants were duly removed from the court and the trial concluded in their absence. In the words of Lewis Carroll:

> *'I'll be judge, I'll be jury, said cunning old Fury;*
> *I'll try the whole cause, and condemn you to death.'*

The trial had lasted for three days. On 5th April 1794 Danton and his fellow accused were taken through a subdued crowd to the guillotine. The priest who had secretly married Danton now kept him secret company, walking through the crowd alongside the tumbril. Danton was the last of the fifteen men to be executed. A witness wrote afterwards, 'Time cannot erase the horrible pantomime from my memory', and he recalled Danton's last words to the executioner: 'Above all, don't forget to show my head to the people: it's worth the trouble.'

When Mirabeau first heard Robespierre speaking, he drily observed: 'That young man will go far – he believes everything he says.' Danton presents us with the opposite case. He used words to meet the needs of the moment. His speeches to the crowds sounded a note of high drama and pointed in one direction, while his conversations behind the scenes pointed in another. The result was that no one could be sure where Danton stood on any given controversy, perhaps not even Danton himself. It is a problem which has dogged biographers and historians, added to by his unsurprising aversion to committing himself to paper. We are left peering into a smokescreen of contradictory utterances on all the major issues of the day, and it is not surprising that he laid himself open to charges of mendacity, conspiracy and betrayal at a time when the virtues of incorruptibility and purity of purpose were being proclaimed by his arch enemies.

His penchant for secrecy was another two-edged sword which eventually swung against him. More than any other revolutionary leader, he believed in negotiating with France's enemies. This laudable pursuit reveals him as an eminently sensible politician who could see the need for a peaceful solution to the revolutionary wars at the end of the day. He entered into secret missions and shady financial dealings which could be to France's benefit, and also, incidentally to his own. Among the many clandestine activities with which he was rumoured to be associated was an attempt to save the king's life. He was honest enough, however, to tell the constitutional monarchist Lameth that 'If I have to give up all hope, I warn you that, since I don't want my head to fall with his, I shall join those who condemn him', which is what he did. When, on 16th January 1793 the vote was taken to determine the king's fate, Danton endorsed the death penalty with one of his ringing phrases: 'The only place to strike kings is on the head'.

The waters of his financial dealings were every bit as murky as those of his political dealings. Never one to deny himself the good things in life, he left behind him a trail of suspicious transactions which laid him open to accusations that he had been siphoning off public funds, stealing war trophies and receiving bribes. He sidestepped demands to explain the absence of his financial records with the excuse that it was drastic action that was called for in a time of crisis, not petty accounting. Danton was a pragmatic politician whose venality and corruption, if proved in today's world, would probably have earned him no more than loss of office or a term in prison. In the heat of the Revolution, however, his financial transgressions proved to be another nail in his coffin. When the time came to destroy him they were seized on by Robespierre and his other enemies and compounded with his propensity for cloak and dagger politics into the more sinister charges of royalism and treason.

Danton was not obsessed with power. He fought to achieve it and relished the taste of it once he had gained it, but he had no wish to cling to it. He was more interested in reaping the material rewards which came with power. One gets the impression that he wanted nothing more than for the Revolution to end and for France to become a normal society living at peace with its neighbours, so that he could return to his family in his native Champagne and live out his days in mellow affluence as a retired elder statesman. In the words of the historian Norman Hampson,

> [Danton] was, by temperament, a political manager of a kind that is fairly common today, caught in a revolutionary situation where it was necessary to pretend that every issue was an apocalyptic battle between good and evil and every compromise was some sort of treason. He too could speak that kind of language when he had to, but he did it without much conviction.

His lack of conviction deprived him of the killer instinct necessary to survive in the fight to the death which the Revolution imposed on its leaders. Despite the hyperbole of his public language he did not believe in consigning people to the guillotine. He preferred to play a double game, raising the temperature with his rhetoric, then standing back from the consequences. This he managed either by disappearing from the scene or indignantly disclaiming responsibility when bloodshed occurred. In the early stages of the Revolution his ambiguous approach to violence and his generous nature had won him friends and earned him the reputation of a moderate. As the violence of the Revolution increased in intensity this ambiguity could not be sustained. Like the other leaders of the Revolution he was torn apart through the basic fault line in his personality. Attacked as a moderate for his generosity and as a terrorist for his lip-service to violence, he too became isolated, hunted down and destroyed.

Danton had the insight to realize that success in a time of Revolution means becoming a hero, failure turns one into a criminal. His revolutionary passion was tempered by a shrewd grasp of reality. He was not interested in chasing the dream of Jean Jacques Rousseau. What he really wanted was to live a comfortable life, inhale the air of his native countryside and bask in the love of his adoring family. But he underestimated the power of the people who embraced him as their leader. He had plunged into the Revolution with the same impetuousness with which, as a boy, he had plunged into the river Aube. Unfortunately the Revolution was no river to be dipped into. It was more like quicksand, pulling him in deeper and finally sucking him under.

CHAPTER FOUR

Violence and Enlightenment
The Paradox of the French Revolution

'Nobody expects the Spanish Inquisition!'
Monty Python

Nobody expected a revolution in France in 1789. The suffering of the common people had been endemic for centuries, but it had largely been a silent suffering. The bitterness and hatred which had been eating its way into society like a disease had found no outward expression. True, there had been rumblings of discontent and grievance for most of the eighteenth century, but these went unheard except by a handful of philosophers and lawyers who struggled to articulate them and give them coherence. Two hidden forces were at work, the build-up of anger which would explode into violence and the flow of enlightened thinking which would give the violence a voice while at the same time raising hopes for a better world.

The sequence of events in a revolution is roughly as follows: A mass of disaffected people combine forces to make an assault on a tyrannical regime. At first the tyrants stand their ground but sooner or later they give way and are either imprisoned, driven into exile or killed. Violence is an intrinsic part of the process of revolution but so is a radical restructuring of the political architecture. New minds get to work to fashion a new society out of new ideas. The prospect of writing on a *tabula rasa* creates a wave of euphoria. There is unanimity of purpose but this collapses under the realization that old structures cannot be so easily obliterated and that old problems do not magically disappear. Different factions emerge, each purporting to represent the best interests of the society.

Following the acute outbreak of violence a struggle for power ensues. Would-be leaders enter the power vacuum created by the annihilation of the original power base. The violence continues until the populace grows tired and settles for peace and stability over and above the quest for a perfect solution. Even then, the violence is never fully extinguished and the cycle is at risk of being repeated. 'When you undertake to run a revolution,' said Mirabeau, 'the difficulty is not to make it go; it is to hold it in check.'

The revolutionary drama can be translated into a few simple emotional constructs. Hatred and fear are the predisposing elements to the violence which results in the overthrow of the ruling tyranny. Counter-violence sets up a vicious cycle of fear, revenge and retaliation. Violence results in both physical and mental trauma. The sense of a process becoming out of control, together with feelings of chaos and instability are as much a cause of fear as the violence itself. One solution to this is the imposition of order and control, effected by ruthless legislation and widespread policing.

The combination of trauma and pre-existing hatred compounds the violence and drives people into defensive groupings in which they feel emotionally and intellectually justified in their self-protective stances. They also feel safe enough within their chosen fortresses to attack those who threaten their integrity. 'Inside' and 'outside' become important constructs and each group is at pains to define itself and the other groups in such terms. 'Inside' comes to be represented as 'good' and 'outside' as 'bad.' Paranoid thinking takes over and fear, which is often accompanied by feelings of helplessness, is replaced by terror, a weapon designed to bring about submission.

The explosion of the French Revolution, when it finally came, produced a seismic shock, a societal big bang, which broke up the political landscape of Europe and changed its face forever. An old world had fallen to pieces, and even before the dust had settled a new world was rising shakily in its place, like a newly hatched creature which nobody could identify but which some proclaimed as a god, others as a monster.

To the intellectually dilapidated aristocrats who sat pugnaciously at the top of a dwindling pyramid of wealth, the word 'revolution' existed, but it had only a faint resonance for them. Their main concern was to obstruct the king in his effete attempts to rescue France from bankruptcy at their expense. The occasional eruptions of violence in the countryside, driven by hunger and panic, were regarded as the irritating manifestations of a brutish society of peasants for whom there could be no understanding or sympathy and who had to be either crushed or ignored.

The story goes that Louis XVI had to be awakened from his sleep to be given the news that the Bastille had fallen. 'Is it a rebellion?' he asked. 'No, sire', was the reply. 'It is a *revolution*.' The scene has a surreal quality. The king, innocent and bemused, shakes off his drowsiness to find himself, like Rip van Winkle, in a world which he does not recognize. He has to be told by one of his functionaries that his kingdom is about to be overturned, and it is tempting to imagine him sinking back into his bed, pulling the bedclothes over his head and going back to sleep.

To the sleepy monarch a rebellion would have been a minor affair, something to be put down once and for all, a mere matter of calling out the troops to trample over a few bodies and fire a few shots into the crowd. But the big bang which heralded the Revolution did not just subside into a sullen calm. Like an earthquake, it produced a series of after-shocks. The ground continued to shake alarmingly, new cracks appeared and crevices opened up where least expected. It was as if a massive subterranean collision had occurred in a part of the world where it was least expected.

Looked at dispassionately, the concept of revolution implies a rapid and fundamental change in the established order of things. It could apply as much to gardening or dress fashion as to any other group enterprise. In its political meaning, however, it refers to a fundamental change in the way in which society is governed. In this context the word readily becomes infused with a passion which splits society into warring factions. The fundamental issue has always been whether revolution is a step towards progress or the opposite, a breakdown into anarchy. The philosopher Alfred North Whitehead observed that 'the art of progress is to preserve order amid change and to preserve change amid order'. In a time of revolution the difference between change and order is polarized into conflicting ideologies and the language of extremism takes hold. Between the party of order and the party of change there can be no compromise. Stridency and over-simplification carry the day.

The etymology of the word 'revolution' suggests a cyclical process, like the turn of a wheel. Those who have been at the top fall off and those who have been at the bottom are carried to the top. In political terms, an old system of government is replaced by a new one, and in the process the old order is dismantled and a new one constructed. Although a revolution can be in the making for years, perhaps decades, its onset is often dramatic and unexpected, and its course is almost invariably attended by large-scale violence. The change from stability to turbulence takes most people unawares, and nobody quite knows what hidden agencies have caused the wheel to begin to turn in the first place. In emotional terms there has been a massive shock to the body politic.

The tangled debates which surround the French Revolution stem from the apparent contradiction between its violent and enlightened aspects. To most people, violence is abhorrent and the thrust of all humane thinkers is to discover ways of preventing, or at best, containing it. For this to happen, the origins of violence in its different guises have to be understood.

The violence which occurred during the Revolution was similar in some respects to that which stalks today's revolutions. Angry protesting crowds gave license to acts of mayhem perpetrated under the cloak of anonymity. A more insidious form of violence soon developed, sanctioned and orchestrated in advance by groups of politicians and carried out by specially appointed agents under the rubric of some form of judicial, political, or military authority. Such was the violence of the September massacres of 1792 and the Reign of Terror which took hold in 1793 and 1794.

In the cycle of violence causes and consequences are not clearly distinguishable. Calls to violence arose out of mixed motives: In the name of a principle (freedom, equality, justice), as an attack on the symbols of tyranny, or out of a visceral need (the clamour for bread, for example and outrage at the laws governing prices and wages). Later the violence was driven by a paranoid fear of enemy attacks without any clear idea of who the enemy was. Some forms of crowd violence had a relatively innocuous onset such as the search for supplies of flour or arms in the prelude to the fall of the Bastille. The situation could be turned in an instant into a murderous onslaught, the spectacle of which became seared into the memory of the people.

Rage and panic are the most contagious of emotions. When these emotions are aroused in a context of long-standing deprivation, frustration and bitterness violence is a natural outcome. In the French countryside violence was fuelled by rumours of conspiracies and fears of attacks by aristocrats. Later, as the violence mushroomed into civil war, anger and persecutory fears came to the fore.

As new political formations developed, some revolutionaries became bent on repressing the violence, others were determined to exploit it for their own ends. During the second half of the Revolution, the relatively spontaneous, inarticulate crowd violence was given a new purpose by leaders with demagogic skills who provided the intellectual justification for the violence. Their motivation was twofold. Firstly, they feared the fickle and uncontrollable nature of the violence and wanted to stem its tide for their own safety, and secondly, they saw an opportunity to promote their own particular political and philosophical policies by orchestrating the violence against their chosen enemies. As Danton, said, 'We must be terrible in order to prevent the people from being terrible.'

The violence destroyed not only many thousands of lives but cleared away the rotten edifice of the *ancien regime*. It left behind a wasteland which was colonized by idealists and opportunists, all of whom agreed on the end but failed to co-operate. Where the air is foul and stale, every breath becomes an effort. Reflective thinking becomes impossible and it is only the body's reflexes which are at work to maintain life. A fresh current of air allows the mind to think. In France, this fresh current came in the form of the Enlightenment. The Revolution breathed new life into a suffocating organism.

The spirit of the Enlightenment which swept over England and France during the seventeenth and eighteenth centuries dispersed the stagnation which was paralyzing social thought. The spread of new ideas about the nature of man, the place of reason in the scheme of things and the quest for happiness could only happen through the development of a network of communication which could penetrate the isolation of a benighted society. The catalyst for this was the growth of literacy, and with it the proliferation of the printed word. The literature of the *philosophes* seeped into the educational system in the form of novels and philosophical tracts which presented a picture of people as innately virtuous and capable of leading upright lives without recourse to religious dogma or the corrupting influence of a lifestyle based on wealth and artifice.

Disaffection with the church was producing a new breed of human being, those who believed in the power of reason. These intellectual upstarts held that mankind would gain, not only by knowledge which had been revealed in mysterious ways at some point in the distant past and recorded in ancient texts, but by conclusions drawn from what people could observe with their own eyes in the world around them. In the seventeenth century a wave of religious and philosophical enlightenment broke over the shores of Europe.

By this time the watchdogs of religious fundamentalism were too feeble to do much about it. Spinoza could be excommunicated and Descartes could be scolded like a naughty child, but Europe was a big place, and there were enough safe havens for these renegade philosophers to retreat and continue their subversive writings in peace. Their thoughts entered a communication network of educated minds which transcended national boundaries. From there they percolated down to the politicians who translated them into a language which ordinary people could understand. Never mind the fact that some of the translations deviated from the obscure and high flown language of the original treatises. The message that people could shape their own destiny and did not have to lead their lives in the shadow of original sin or fear of eternal damnation was enough to instil hope that a better life could be created in this world without having to wait for the next one. Hope became an overriding emotion in the repertoire of revolutionary sentiments.

From this distance the enlightenment appears like a stream of white light illuminating the darkness of medieval thought. On closer inspection it shows up as a rainbow of diverse viewpoints, many of which were as incompatible with each other as the strands of religious thought which they replaced.

Rousseau, for instance, attached more importance to feelings than to reason. What mattered, he maintained, was what the individual felt to be right. One's conscience could never deceive, whereas reason could be twisted in various ways by powerful groups such as the church to suit their nefarious purposes. For Montesquieu, on the other hand, the matter was not so simple. There were many forces at play in society, church, state and family for example, each of which had a claim on the individual in addition to his free-floating conscience.

Individual will was therefore central to Rousseau's thinking, while for Montesquieu the group was all-important and the individual was merely a nodal point through which numerous circles intersected in a complex and organic society.

This view is remarkably similar to the modern conception of the relationship between individuals and groups elaborated by the twentieth-century psychiatrist, S.H. Foulkes. According to Foulkes, society is made up of a matrix of interpersonal relationships comparable to the networks of interconnected cells in the brain. In this model individuals achieve understanding of their fellow human beings through the flow of communication within and around them. The process goes awry when this flow is impeded, cutting off some individuals from others and surrounding them with a wall of isolation. For Foulkes, isolation was the antithesis of communication, and his practice of psychotherapy within a group setting aimed at the breaking down of pockets of isolation and restoring free-flowing communication by encouraging a climate in which people could talk freely to one another.

The juxtaposition of violence and enlightenment is more easily understood as the start of a vast movement of communication following a long period of cultural isolation. Clumsy, faltering and dangerous, the battles of the French Revolution were fought at both a primitive and an intellectual level. The dangers of this lay in a naïve desire to achieve a unity of purpose without taking into account the differences inherent in the human race. Sustaining the Revolution became a hallowed principle. To disagree with this principle was to betray the Revolution. But how was it possible to get down to the nuts and bolts of the newly designed structure without some measure of civilized disagreement and compromise?

It was this failure to accept the need for constructive debate and co-operation over the details of the revolutionary political structures that turned the revolutionaries into faction fighters, each factional leader claiming possession of the truth and pronouncing the others to be a danger to their particular version of the truth and therefore to the Revolution itself. Only after the fires of internecine violence had burnt themselves out, leaving behind another wasteland, was the ground cleared for a new breed of leader to emerge, a man who believed not in revolutionary ideals but in restored glory and the power of guns. Napoleon Bonaparte's solution to the danger of endemic violence was to harness it into military might and turn it outwards, to the world beyond France.

The revolutionary explosion was the result of a massive collision between two worlds, the old and the new. Each world was made up of groups of people who had lived separate existences from each other for centuries, communicating only in the crude mercenary and legal language necessary to protect wealth and status. Those in power were determined to maintain the existing order and prevent social change. Those without power had no hope of change, only a belief in salvation through faith.

Two separate cultures had evolved, devoid of mutual understanding, empathy or compassion. Aggression between peoples who have become separate from each other is a common story, both before and after the Revolution. Separation leads to isolation, the precursor of violence. Fear, panic and rage in the face of deprivation are the emotions which attend isolation. The combination of these emotions provided the explosive mix which found its outlet in inter-group violence.

In retrospect, the premonitory signs of a revolution were in the air during the year preceding the fall of the Bastille. A cruel winter coupled with a disastrous crop failure in 1788 had resulted in waves of panic and anger sweeping the countryside. Rumours of an aristocratic conspiracy to starve the people led to sporadic violence which was put down, but without any awareness of the impending explosion. Nor was there any centralized machinery for tightening control in the event of more widespread disturbances. It took no more than a single incident, the fall of the Bastille, to provide the touch-paper for the big bang of the French Revolution. In the electric atmosphere which followed, opposition became enmity and the voice of reason was drowned by the roar of passion.

The States General, the national forum through which the king had hoped to bring about peaceful change, imploded almost as soon as it had been convened, and the various assemblies which followed it quickly became emotionally charged platforms from which to level blame for the woes of the people in a language which mirrored the violence of the streets.

A process which began peacefully as a reasoned plea to redress wrongs was undermined, not only by the violence of the disaffected masses but by the intransigence of the king. Between 4th May 1789, the day on which the States General convened, and 14th July 1789, the day on which the Bastille fell, most of the nobility appeared deaf to the long lists of grievances being waved at them. Some absented themselves entirely from the chamber to carry on their political intrigues elsewhere. Others sat through the debates as if in a trance, waiting for the inspired leadership which never came. The unexpected explosion of violence which announced the Revolution produced fright, shock, panic and confusion.

Whenever dangerous emotions come to the surface, the animal brain which lurks in all of us springs into action and blocks the power of rational thought. Decisions are made in a flash, misunderstandings arise just as quickly and violence begets violence. The result is a contagion of violence and a sequence of trauma and counter-violence. The revolutionaries discovered that the fruits of violence were bitter-sweet. They knew that wounds would be inflicted on them, but they experienced far more powerful emotions than the fear of trauma – the thrill of new-found power and the sensation of freedom.

The angry crowds who stormed the Bastille exulted in the realization that their victorious assault had only provoked a weak response. A celebratory sense of people-power took hold which spread like wildfire. Groups of political activists crystallized into extra-parliamentary clubs which became hotbeds of revolutionary debate stirred into a frenzy by radical demagogues. The raw emotions of these early group formations were soon dressed in sophisticated ideological clothing by articulate leaders who came out of the shadows to give direction to the violence. With successive explosions of violence, the myth of a sublime unity fractured, the parties in conflict polarized, and the middle ground fell away.

═ ❖ ═

The French were by no means the first to stage a political revolution. Nearly a century and a half earlier the English had overthrown their king and replaced him, if only for a few years, with a government by the people. And forty years after that the term 'revolution' was applied to another upheaval in England when the Catholic James II was deposed and replaced on the throne by the Protestant Dutch ruler William III and his wife Mary, in what came to be known as the 'Glorious Revolution' of 1688.

But this was a relatively minor affair which, though not entirely a 'bloodless' revolution, as it has been called, simply resulted in a further lurch in power away from the monarchy towards parliament without tearing apart the fabric of society. And in 1783, after a struggle lasting eight years, the American Colonies successfully threw off their British rulers and established themselves as an independent nation. All of these earlier revolutions gave ideas to the enlightened thinkers and politicians of the day about ways in which society could change, but none of them had as much impact on the way in which people lived their lives or thought about society as the French Revolution.

The question must be asked: 'Why France, of all countries?' After all, there were other European countries which were more deeply mired in the barbaric traditions of the feudal age. Despite the country's downward economic spiral, the degradation and oppression of the lower strata of French Society was of a lesser order than that of its Austrian and Prussian neighbours. Yet, paradoxically, this relative release from the extremes of drudgery, tyranny and physical hardship created the collective state of mind which hastened the advent of the Revolution. People were able to think.

Before the Revolution France was a relatively stable society which had coalesced into three main social groups: The aristocracy, the common people and the clergy. The aristocracy, buffered from economic decline and famine by a thicket of entrenched privileges, were united by the myth that they were descended from ancestors whose right to rule had been given to them by God and was transmitted down the generations by ties of blood.

The common people, encompassing the vast majority of France's twenty-six million inhabitants, were a heterogeneous group united mainly by their adherence to the Catholic faith and by their exclusion from aristocratic privilege with all the hardships and obstacles to personal advancement which this exclusion entailed. The status of this group had remained unchanged since feudal times when it had been stamped with the identity of a Third Estate of the realm (beneath the aristocracy as the Second Estate and the clergy as the First Estate). An iniquitous and ramshackle set of laws and taxes kept the Third Estate in their place, closest to the soil and furthest from God's unconditional benevolence.

The clergy mirrored the split which divided the privileged from the unprivileged. The higher clergy enjoyed an immunity from taxation and a protected lifestyle as did some of the clergy who lived and worked on the considerable areas of land owned by the church. On the other hand, many of the parish priests in the towns and villages lived modest lives and tended to identify with the suffering of the common people whom they served. When the Revolution came, this division would widen into a gulf, forcing all clergy to choose between allegiance to the new revolutionary constitution or the Church of Rome. Those who opted for the latter soon found themselves deemed unpatriotic and alien, along with the aristocrats, and either forced into emigration or subjected to humiliating prohibitions which culminated in a frontal attack on Christianity as the Revolution metamorphosed into the Terror.

This bird's-eye-view of pre-revolutionary France as three estates divided by privilege into two large groups demarcates the central fault-line along which France split when the Revolution broke. If we zoom in on each of these groups a more complex configuration of sub-groups appears, each with its own separate identity. We see France as a largely agrarian society which had not yet been touched by the indus-trial and technological advances already strengthening the British economy. The majority of the Third Estate were peasant farmers who worked the land using primitive methods of agriculture which increased their privation when times were bad.

A smaller sub-group of the Third Estate clustered in the cities and towns. These were the shopkeepers, artisans, merchants and traders who catered to the everyday needs of the populace. This sub-group, like the clergy, split into two with the advent of the Revolution. Those living in Paris joined forces with disaffected residents from the poorer quarters of the city to form a militant group of political activists known as the *sans-culottes*, named for the fact that they wore trousers instead of the aristocratic *culottes* or breeches. This new group became the standard bearers and watchdogs of the Revolution, proudly modeling in their customs and habits the modest lifestyle proclaimed as virtuous by revolutionary ideologues.

The relatively prosperous members of the Third Estate, especially those living in centres of commerce with ready access to trading ports like Marseilles, or towns where there was a thriving textile industry like Lyons, had the most to lose from an assault on privilege. When the Revolution came, bringing with it the collapse of the aristocracy, this group, with its ambivalent attitude towards the great levelling operation fanning out across the country from Paris, became a hive of counter-revolutionary activity and a target of bitter revolutionary hostility. The result was yet another polarized configuration of groups, corresponding roughly to a Paris-centred group bent on accelerating the process of change, and a group distributed more widely through the provinces, where efforts to slow down or even reverse the process of change were concentrated.

Social isolation cuts people off from reality and predisposes them to paranoia. Similarly, when groups become isolated, as is the case with religious cults or political groups operating in secret, we can trace a chain of mental events in which the self-imposed isolation of the group nurtures false assumptions about the 'Other'. This hardens prejudiced thinking and ultimately fosters delusional beliefs.

All groups retain a shared memory bank of experiences, beliefs, images and myths from which they retrieve information. This is necessary if a group is to grow and maintain its integrity. A group which sequesters itself from the wider society looks inwardly for direction and inspiration. It seeks guidance from charismatic leaders on whom the members become dependent.

Good and evil become polarized into antagonistic forces. Freedom of thought is discouraged and blind obedience becomes the order of the day. 'Good' powers may be invoked by acts of appeasement such as scapegoating, offering sacrifices and adhering to rituals designed to gain protection. These devices are designed to keep 'evil' powers at bay and drive incipient 'evil' forces out of the group.

Isolated individuals form unrealistic views of the world, based more on perceptions drawn from the imagination than exchanges with others. The window of a submarine looks out on a sea of darkness which takes on fantastic shapes created in the mind of the viewer and given life by being projected into the darkness. If there is limited or no communication with the outside world these perceptions grow into assumptions which harden into convictions without the benefit of reality testing. These convictions, based on flimsy evidence, are nursed by fantasies of a perfect union within the group in the face of hostility from the outside.

Many of the leaders of the Revolution came from a professional and educated background. These were the administrators, lawyers, and officials who had struggled to uphold the old system while clawing their way up the ladder of personal advancement towards the ceiling of aristocratic privilege. In the decades leading up to the Revolution, this element of the Third Estate had evolved into a disaffected middle class, or bourgeoisie.

It counted among its number many of the articulate thinkers who would provide the intellectual ammunition for the Revolution as well as its political leadership. As revolutionary activity became more extreme, group leaders whose personalities matched these extreme tendencies came to the fore. Some of these were emotionally isolated individuals whose powerful attachment to revolutionary ideals gave them no room to manoeuvre within a network of flesh-and-blood. These were the fanatics and idealists, of whom Robespierre was the most prominent, trapped in a primitive, fused relationship with an abstraction – the Revolution – with which they identified in an almost psychotic way.

These men who led the Revolution were powerful characters, but the political groups of which they were the leaders and by which they were ultimately brought down had a life of their own and even greater power, and the social forces surrounding those groups were even more powerful. Where, then, was the ultimate power located which drove the Revolution? The question may also be asked whether history is shaped by forces which transcend the individual, or whether it the individual who is master of his destiny and whether Carlyle's view that history is simply biography writ large is closer to the truth.

Perhaps the answer lies somewhere between these two romantic notions. The emotional needs of a group seem to find expression in one leader (or a few leaders) with a talent for reading the mind of that group, perhaps because their emotions resonate with those of the leaders. Such people are capable of rendering the demands of the group into a language which can be understood by the wider society. They become invested by their groups with the garments of power and it is only when the group perceives that their idol has clay feet that the relationship between the leader and the led runs into trouble.

Groups have the capacity to impose their will on the wider society. The individuals in the groups have minds of their own, but they are also influenced by the group mind, and in turn, they influence it. Change comes about through a kaleidoscopic re-configuration of power alignments between individuals, groups and society at large, not through a mystical struggle between individual will and the force of destiny. Our understanding of the French Revolution has to take account of the communication between these three elements of the human condition.

It is this power to communicate which liberates us from our animal past. As human beings we have certain attributes which distinguish us from other animals – the capacity to think reflectively, symbolize, communicate through speech and change ourselves as a species by re-modeling our physical environment. But we are constantly at risk of being dragged back to our animal origins by our tendency to fall prey to primitive emotions and hard-wired reflex actions. It is these which come into play when we are faced with new or unexpected, natural forces which bewilder or frighten us. Communication is the only means at our disposal for liberating ourselves from the thrall of our instincts. Through communication we are able to expand our aware-ness of the world around us and co-operate with our fellow human beings in order to meet our collective needs. When communication breaks down isolation sets in and groups close in on themselves.

When the survival of the individual or the group is at stake the mind falls back on more instinctive patterns of thought designed to defend the self and attack the perceived source of danger. In the isolated mind, flashpoints are reached more quickly. Surges of fear trigger the impulse to act violently or flee in terror. Communication acts as a brake on these tendencies. Without its tempering effect there can be no slowing down of the brain's insistent call to answer to the law of the jungle.

While tension was growing among the isolated masses, insidious changes were taking place in the higher echelons of French society. The privileged world of the French aristocracy was being eroded by a mixture of bribery, corruption and legal loopholes. Some of the wealthier, more enterprising elements of the common people had managed to buy their way into the ranks of the nobility, while some of the aristocrats, especially those reliant on income from primitive agriculture, found themselves sliding down a slippery slope towards poverty. The boundaries between the two groups which were destined to collide were slowly, imperceptibly becoming less rigid.

Groups with permeable boundaries grow and flourish through exchange. Despite the economic permeability between the two groups, wealth flowed in only one direction, away from the less well off to the more well off, and the reins of power remained firmly in the hands of the latter, a system reinforced through aristocratic cabals known as *parlements,* which bore no resemblance to a cen-tralized democratic parliament. With France on the verge of bankruptcy the ruling aristocrats closed ranks and exercised their power to protect their own privileges by delaying and obstructing the king in his efforts to extract tax concessions from them. By the mid-dle of 1788 France had reached a state of economic deadlock and social stagnation. There were few exchanges across the boundaries which partitioned the social, cultural, political, administrative or military spheres unless they served the purpose of perpetuating the old system. All avenues for advancement were blocked, resulting in a build-up of dynamic energy. Translated into psychological terms, this became the pent-up rage and frustration which was to find expression in the Revolution as mass violence.

A two-pronged attack on the aristocracy and the church by the leaders of the Enlightenment was met by feeble attempts at censorship which were easily frustrated by the wiles of writers, publishers and booksellers. Works of fiction and philosophy were added to by essays and political treatises which posed uncomfortable questions about the rights of man and the best way to govern society. Rousseau's book, *The Social Contract*, which argued that society could be trusted to rule itself without the loss of individual freedom, was hungrily swallowed by educated revolutionaries like Robespierre, Sièyes and Mirabeau who immediately set about translating it into practical politics. From the 1750s until the outbreak of the Revolution there was a steady outpouring of seditious literature which provided revolutionary ideologues with their intellectual ammunition. The ideas of the Enlightenment soon leapt from the printed page into the speeches being declaimed in the halls of the National Assembly and the political clubs and on the streets of Paris.

Metaphors of death and images of stagnation and fossilization come readily to mind when we think about the reasons for the collapse of the Old Regime. In biological terms, death ensues when there is no longer any exchange of vital materials between an organism and the world which envelopes it. Eventually the body decays and becomes indistinguishable from the environment. A skeletal remnant may be the only reminder that it once existed. The Old Regime was dying, but it was refusing to lie down and turn its face to the wall. The French Revolution was a collision, not only between isolated social groups but between a dying world and a newborn one. The dying world, resistant to change and propped up by ossified institutions, had become entrenched in its feudal culture. The newborn world suffered its baptism of fire, but survived.

In a state of isolation a desert of ignorance often lies between 'us' and 'them', whoever 'they' and 'we' are. In pre-revolutionary France ignorance on the part of the aristocracy about their lowly fellow countrymen bred an attitude of disdain, a view that there was a category of humans who were intrinsically inferior. The resentment which this bred found expression in an undiscriminating apportionment of blame by the majority towards all who were perceived as oppressors, which came to mean all who were not like them. The combination of mutual ignorance based on isolation, and resentment based on an oppressive master–servant relationship provided the ingredients for the violence that shook France and the world in 1789.

If we think of a revolution as an event which marks the point of change between an old order of society and a new one, we can see the French Revolution as a mutative event in the political sphere comparable to the Renaissance in the cultural sphere and the Reformation in the religious sphere. The institutions which preceded the French Revolution vanished and those which followed it were based on entirely new principles of government. Mankind had taken a giant step forward, and although there were convulsive attempts to return to the past in the decades that followed the Revolution, the world would never again be the same. A new spirit of community had come into being, with a new repertoire of emotions at its disposal in the shape of altruism, empathy and mutual identification with one's fellow humans. In the political sphere, a new force – the common people – had found its voice and would have to be reckoned with in all future struggles for power.

The French Revolution marked the beginning of a process, the end-point of which has been difficult to determine. The shape which the Revolution has given to the societies which followed it can be compared to the effect on the animal kingdom of a new life form branching out from the evolutionary tree. New and infinitely complex possibilities for societal change arose from it, and there is still division around the conundrum of whether the Revolution was a signpost to a higher form of society or a throwback to barbarism. The question remains whether society, with all the boosts and benefits of modern-day technology, has progressed or regressed since the big bang of 1789.

Emotions continue to run high on the subject, fuelled by ammunition from political ideologies of both the Left and the Right, but the jury is still out. At this point the often-quoted observation of Zhou En-Lai deserves another airing. When asked by Henry Kissinger, what he thought was the significance of the French Revolution, he replied (and we can imagine a laconic smile) 'It's too soon to say'.

CHAPTER FIVE

The Revolutionary Crowd
Bloodthirsty Mob or Will of the People?

*'I have a horror of crowds. I cannot go into a theatre or watch a public
festival. They fill me with a strange and unbearable unease, a
frightful distress, as if I were struggling might and main
against an irresistible and mysterious power. And indeed,
I am struggling against the soul of the crowd,
which is trying to enter me.'*
Guy de Maupassant

Guy de Maupassant's emotional response to crowds testifies to a universal experience of being pushed and pulled by some powerful force emanating from the crowd. Attraction and repulsion co-exist, generating a *frisson,* a tingling sensation of fear and fascination which precedes any intellectual awareness of the nature and purpose of the crowd.

The crowd exercises its pull by tapping into the primitive mind of the individual and the group. By the same token there is a contrary repulsion driven by the primitive fear of being caught up in danger. The combination of these emotions leads to a general quickening of the senses, a state of arousal which puts the individual on full alert. One reason for this is that crowds are unpredictable. An angry crowd is prone to violence. This in turn provokes panic, creating a vicious cycle. It is by no means clear which way the violence will turn or who will end up as a casualty. When panic occurs it displaces the calmness which is needed for rational judgment. A panic-stricken crowd is as close to group mindlessness as it is possible to get, and the prospect of facing a body of people driven predominantly by panic and rage is terrifying for anyone to contemplate.

Between 1789 and 1794 there were two non-militarized weapon-wielding groups making a bid for power, the Parisian *sans-culottes* and the peasants in the countryside. At first these groups found a common enemy in the aristocracy. But after this category of enemy had been rendered powerless the Paris crowd swelled the ranks of the new national army and proceeded to menace those among the revolutionary leadership who were inclined towards compromise or moderation. Their brethren in the countryside resisted attempts by the revolutionary government to drag them away from the land and into the army to fight the Revolution's wars. Moreover many of them had strong religious sentiments and resented the Revolution's systematic demolition of their beloved Church. The fracture in revolutionary unity which had begun with divided opinions on how to deal with France's external enemies now extended across the country into a Civil War. Revolutionary politicians who had once been comrades-in-arms found themselves driven into opposite camps.

The eruption of sporadic violence provoked a struggle to gain control over the Paris crowd. In the all-or-nothing mentality which prevails when violence splits a group, each political faction strove to demonstrate loyalty to the people in order to avoid being cast as an enemy of the Revolution. But who exactly constituted the people? And was the violence of the Paris crowd an expression of the will of the people, or was it an aberration which could not be contained by civilized debate? Could violence only be met by be counter-violence?

The political power of the *sans-culottes* who controlled the Paris crowd forced the politicians to adopt increasingly ferocious measures against the alleged enemies of the Revolution in order to stay in control. Inside the assembly the language of the debates was wild, the arguments punctuated by invective, accusations and threats. Outside the assembly the waves of crowd violence which battered against its doors and occasionally washed into the chamber itself led to tense confrontations between the deputies and the deputations of citizens who gathered with impunity at the foot of the podium, interrupting the work of the assembly.

Crowd power extracted placatory concessions and weakened the legislature. There was no army at hand to protect the sacrosanct process of parliamentary democracy and it was only after the fall of Robespierre, when Napoleon Bonaparte decided that there could be no place for armed throngs of citizens in the decision-making processes of the republic and blasted them with gunfire, that the crowd lost its power as a political force. With Napoleon's act of bloodshed a different order of violence came into its own and the army regained its ascendancy as the principal agent of power.

Since crowd violence was an intrinsic part of the French Revolution it is impossible to treat the subject of the Revolution as a political movement without taking a position on the degree to which it influenced the course of the Revolution.

It is difficult to be objective about riots and mayhem. If a historian or politician is in sympathy with the cause behind such turbulence, the crowd is presented as the legitimate expression of protest or an outcry against tyranny. On the other hand, if the establishment is seen as undeserving of its fate, the crowd is presented as a primitive, dangerous and destructive force.

In the case of the French Revolution, one view holds that the violence of the crowd was the inevitable outcome of centuries of oppression, that it accounted for only a small proportion of the casualties and that it was the only means by which the despotic power of the day could be shaken and toppled from its edifice.

The opposing voice argues that reforms were imminent anyway, that the established order was already rotten and dying on its feet, and that the violence of the crowd, whatever its origins, was a gratuitous expression of all that is worst in human nature, a throwback to barbarism and animal behaviour. According to this view, the violence of the crowd was unleashed because the ruling powers were too weak to maintain law and order, and the lesson to be learnt was that the masses had to be controlled with an iron fist if the horrors of revolution were to be avoided.

Each side of this divide presented its case in language designed to bolster its case. Revolutionary propaganda played down the violent acts of revolutionaries, highlighted the cruelty and injustices perpetrated by their adversaries and steered the argument towards the beneficial social changes wrought by revolution. Anti-Revolutionary propaganda down the ages embroidered the imagery of crowd violence, portraying it in lurid detail and justifying the need to control it, by force if necessary.

Exaggeration and caricature were used as weapons by both sides. Popular narratives of the Revolution were (and are) usually illustrated by at least one or two pictures of a mob in full flood. In some scenes our gaze is drawn to decapitated heads held aloft on pikes. In others, the crowd is being fired on by soldiers, or perhaps the soldiers themselves are being massacred amidst general mayhem. Everywhere we look people are being assaulted, dragged to their deaths, shot at close range, hacked to pieces or strung up on lampposts. These are the traumatic images of the Revolution which have been etched into our collective memory and they pose an uncomfortable question: Are such acts necessary before mankind can be liberated?

But while headlines scream and distort one way or the other, the dispassionate observer is more interested in balancing the social and political context of crowd behavior against the spectacle of its traumatizing scenes. To this person the crowd is seen as only one element in a complex field which deserves more detailed analysis than can be conveyed by graphic and simplistic images.

The sad truth is that violence between groups is endemic in the human race. The violence of the revolutionary crowd is no different in kind to that which has characterized every battle or massacre before or since the French Revolution. The killing of others on a large scale has been variously interprcted as defensive or aggressive, criminal or glorious, redeeming or damnable.

At the end of the day it does not make too much difference whether you are killed by a butcher's knife, a soldier's sword or a blast of gunfire, whether your last moments are spent in the heat of battle, at the hands of a mob or as a prisoner being led to the scaffold. The distinction between a rioting crowd, a terrorist group or an army unit should not be made on the basis of uniforms, flags or the lack of them, but on the ethical and legal principles upheld or breached by these groups.

There was, however, one important difference between the Paris crowd and its pre-revolutionary predecessors. The crowds who stormed the Bastille and then a few weeks later triumphantly escorted the king from Versailles into virtual captivity in Paris presented the world with its first example of a successful civilian crowd, a group with no military status on the march to political power. Before that, the uprisings and rebellions which had erupted on the European landscape from time to time had been small, chaotic affairs, easily quelled by disciplined troops loyal to the powers of the day. Now, for the first time, a crowd discovered that it was unstoppable and that it was a political force to be reckoned with.

The monarchy failed to realize that the soldiers who guarded it were also people, fuelled by the same frustrations as those who pressed against them. With the advent of crowd power the boundary between the army and the people fell away. The king came to rely increasingly on foreign troops for his safety, while a new military leadership sprang up, out of nowhere, it seemed, which began moulding the raw material of the crowd into a new body of armed citizens. Officers with

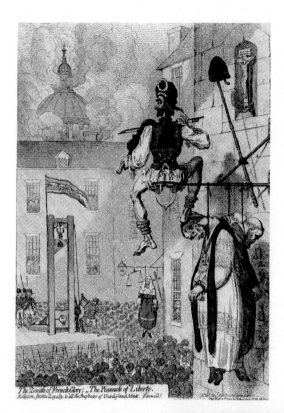

The Execution of Louis XVI on 21st January 1793. The English cartoonist James Gillray captured the mood of revulsion which greeted the king's execution in a country already shaken by the violence of the Revolution.

Louis XVI (1754 – 1793), King of France from 1774. He was devoted to his family and appalled at the prospect of shedding French blood. His weakness and vacillation fed into the forces of the Revolution which eventually destroyed him.

An Unholy Trinity: George-Jacques Danton (1759 – 1794), Jean Paul Marat (1743 – 1793) and Maximilien de Robespierre (1758 – 1794). Three radical revolutionary leaders who unleashed the Terror. They have become etched into the public consciousness as either demons or heroes in a world still divided about the Revolution itself.

So Near and Yet So Far. Louis XVI and his family detained at Varennes near the Austrian border. Their attempted escape from France in June 1791 led to a sea-change in the public mood towards the monarchy.

March of the Women on Versailles, 5th October 1789. Spearheaded by the market-women of Paris, an angry crowd made its way to Versailles, broke into the palace and forced the royal family to return to Paris under escort.

Marie Antoinette caricatured as a leopard -like beast. The royal family were often portrayed as animals or monsters. The inscription mockingly refers to the queen as the Baroness de Korff, a false identity she assumed during the flight from Paris.

The Execution of Danton and Desmoulins on 5th April 1794. Desmoulins' childhood friendship with Robespierre gave him no immunity after his repeated attacks on Robespierre in speeches and articles. Danton's ranting eloquence at his own trial was to no avail. His last words were addressed to the executioner: 'Make sure you show my head to the people. It's worth a look.'

Jacques Pierre Brissot (1754 – 1793), a leading Girondin and fervent advocate of war with Austria and Prussia as the way to save the Revolution. A bitter enemy of Robespierre, he was executed with twenty other Girondins on 31st October 1793.

The adolescent Robespierre in the aristocratic attire which was to characterize his appearance throughout the Revolution.

'ANOTHER ONE!'

Mirror Image. Robespierre 'the Incorruptible' saw enemies everywhere, getting in the way of his ideal Revolution.

aristocratic credentials were culled and their places taken by soldiers who were inspired by revolutionary ideology. Generals were given the Herculean task of fusing the new troops with the old and motivating them to fight for the revolutionary cause.

This new citizens' army was the nucleus around which the most formidable fighting force in Europe would grow. But before that could happen, a fight to the death had broken out between rival politicians trying to hold on to power. Survival meant keeping control of the crowd, and this could only be done either by appeasing the beast, by outdoing it in violence by throwing it sacrificial victims – this was the radical solution – or by attacking those identified as its leaders and making a moral appeal over the heads of the crowd to the people at large to respect the power of the law. This was the moderate solution, doomed to fail because the crowd sensed its own power and the weakness of its adversaries. Fine words cast as brilliant rhetoric could not prevail over the passions unleashed by brute force.

The confusion which has bedeviled our understanding of crowd behaviour stems from the fact that the crowd is not only a 'thing', a phenomenon to be studied like a nest of ants, but a symbol which stirs passions and carries meaning. A symbol is a shared fantasy which serves to unify a group. The fantasy crystallizes into a belief about the thing which it represents. Once the thing itself (the crowd in this case) has been invested with symbolic significance its true nature becomes obscured and its symbolic associations take over. The symbolic object continues to attract emotional charges and becomes a target for projected wishes and fears. It comes to acquire a value for good or bad and enters the network of communication which makes up the social matrix. Here it comes into contact with ideas which either reinforce or challenge the qualities with which it has been endowed.

The social mind is a network in a constant state of dynamic flux. It works and plays with symbols, modelling them into diverse shapes, shading them in and investing them with particular emotions. In the evolving context of society the crowd as a symbol can be transformed from something good into something bad, or the transformation might occur in the reverse direction. 'There's nothing either good or bad but thinking makes it so'.

The importance of the social context in shaping a symbol is nicely illustrated by another iconic image of the Revolution, the guillotine. Like the crowd, the guillotine has come to symbolize the violent nature of the Revolution. Yet when this contraption first appeared against the skyline it was hailed as a humane way of avoiding the brutal and botched methods of doing people to death which preceded it.

Dr Joseph Guillotin, the man who refined it from an earlier model, (and who, by the way, deplored the fact that it carried his name along with the opprobrium which attached to it), regarded it as a gesture towards the Enlightenment. It was to be the great equalizer, an instrument which would draw no distinction between the final moments of aristocrats and those of the common people. As the Revolution turned into the Terror, the guillotine, like the crowd, lost its benign aura and took on the aspect of a monstrous killing machine. Today, along with the pikestaffs and pitchforks of the mob, it has taken its place among the exhibits in the Revolution's Chamber of Horrors.

Both sides in the revolutionary conflict needed symbolic acts as well as objects to capture the essence of what they were fighting for. They needed symbols which could clearly and simply represent not only their own struggle but the dark forces of the enemy. Because the Revolution was, in essence, a violent conflict, partisans on both sides of the divide seized what evidence they could from every act of violence to strengthen their case.

This meant that all acts of violence on the part of counter-revolutionaries were invoked to justify revolutionary violence and *vice versa*. In this war of symbols decapitation would come to symbolize the destruction of the monarchy, but before this association had been consciously made, the spectacle of the mob parading its grisly trophies through the streets fused the image of the crowd with the image of decapitation. This led to a chain of associations which turned the crowd into a symbol of revolutionary barbarism, and then by a process of elision into a symbol of the Revolution itself.

No better example exists of the discrepancy between the symbol and the thing itself than the Bastille, an enormous fortress with eight towers and eighty-foot high walls, built in the fourteenth century. By 1789 it had become a hollow shell of a prison, earmarked for demolition. In the minds of Parisians, however, it was a symbol of the *ancien regime*, a place where victims of the regime were tortured, incarcerated and left to die in horrible conditions. The discovery of only a handful of prisoners living in conditions which compared favourably with those of other Paris prisons did nothing to shake the symbolic significance with which it had been invested.

Frustrated by the absence of a visible body in Paris to hear its protest and lacking in both leadership and sense of direction, the crowd, like a headless monster, turned its attention to the search for arms. Suddenly the hated Bastille loomed large, not only as a reminder of the people's suffering but as a storehouse of weapons and ammunition. The original intention was simply to demand these commodities, not to occupy or destroy the building.

The crowd around the Bastille lacked leadership, but so too did the small band of officers in charge of the Bastille, a Dad's Army of pensioners led by the prison's nervous and indecisive governor, de Launay. This unfortunate man created confusion by simultaneously offering to accede to the demands of the crowd and threatening to blow up the Bastille. Officers of the Paris Town Hall tried to mediate but their efforts failed because their talks with the governor took so long that the restive crowd assumed that they had been detained against their will.

This misunderstanding was followed by others. The governor's peaceful gesture of removing the cannons which were pointing menacingly at the crowd was seen as a sign that they being withdrawn to be loaded in readiness for firing into the crowd. When he finally wrote a note of surrender he had no means of communicating it to the crowd, and the situation became hopeless when his order to lower the drawbridge resulted in some of the besiegers being crushed. Shooting began and the inflamed crowd poured into the building, bent not only on the search for supplies but on revenge for their fallen comrades.

In practical terms the overthrow of the Bastille did no more than empty out the building and hasten its demolition. As a symbolic victory, however, its significance was tremendous. The sheer unexpectedness of its fall created a sense of triumph and euphoria that reverberated through France and made governments elsewhere sit up and take notice.

The revolutionaries reached a simple conclusion: If a large number of poorly armed people could prevail against a well-armed force occupying a mighty fortress there was no reason why such a feat could not be repeated against any other force bristling with guns and hiding behind thick walls. The fall of the Bastille introduced the people to itself, not only as a theoretical concept in revolutionary doctrine, but as a powerful weapon in the shape of the crowd.

Those who were at the centre of the successful assault on the Bastille were hailed as the Revolution's first heroes. They were awarded the title 'Conqueror of the Bastille' and given certificates recording the gratitude of the people for having brought about 'the triumph of liberty over despotism'. The murder and decapitation of some of the surrendered officers who had been responsible for the defence of the

Bastille, including the wretched de Launay, were dismissed as acts of justified rage. An atmosphere of riotous celebration took hold of the populace, and the fourteenth of July 1789 entered history as the beginning of a new era.

Ten weeks after the fall of the Bastille the crowd found another opportunity to test its newly discovered power. The king was still prevaricating at Versailles, egged on to intransigence by an aristocratic clique who had trampled, literally and figuratively, on the revolutionary cockade. The view took hold among the people that the king's rightful place was in Paris, surrounded by his subjects. In symbolic terms, the head of France remained disconnected from its heart, and that would not do if the body politic were to pulsate as one. So, if the king would not come to Paris, Paris would have to come to the king.

On 5th October 1789 a large crowd led by a phalanx of women set out on the thirteen-mile road to Versailles. Trailing behind them was the newly formed National Guard under the uncertain leadership of Lafayette, with a vague brief to maintain order. True to his inclination to avoid bloodshed at all costs, Louis tried to placate the vanguard of the crowd. He agreed to meet a delegation of six women, to whom he uttered soothing promises to resolve the bread crisis and sign the Declaration of Rights.

The calm produced by this sop did not last, however. Drink, hunger, frustration and exhaustion provided an explosive mix. The inadequately guarded palace was breached and the crowd spilled into the inner chambers of the royal family. Marie Antoinette was moments away from being set upon and only managed to save herself by hurrying down a secret corridor to her husband's bedroom. Louis, penned in by the crowd, tried his royal magic once again and reassured them that their demands would be met.

This roller-coaster confrontation between the people and the monarch went on through the night and into the next day. Lafayette, still trading on his popularity as France's soldier hero of the American War of Independence, persuaded Louis that his only way out was to accede to the crowd's demands that the royal family should leave Versailles at once and take up residence in the Tuileries, a rundown palace in the heart of Paris. So began the first of the two humiliating coach journeys to Paris which announced to the world that the French royal family were effectively prisoners of their own people. They would make the second journey after their recapture at Varennes in 1791, where once again the crowd would take them into its custody and ensure that there could be no rescue by remnants of the king's loyal troops.

An important sideshow to the incursion at Versailles was the infiltration by the crowd into the hall in which the deputies of the National Assembly were arguing the issues of the day. Here they mingled provocatively with the deputies and shouted down the speakers. When the president tried to call them to order he was greeted with cries of 'We don't give a fuck for order!' 'We want bread!' and told that his head would shortly be used as the ball in a ball-game.

A prescient observer might have discerned in this scene the beginnings of the revolutionary conflict between parliamentary and extra-parliamentary democracy. The sacred boundary separating the elected representatives of the people from the people themselves had been breached. From now on there would be a constant tension between those who saw direct action as the solution to France's problems and those who believed in delegated authority.

Until the march on Versailles, power had been see-sawing between the Monarchy and the deputies of the National Assembly. With the forced return of the royal family to Paris the crowd had shown itself as a third force in this power struggle. The leaders of the Revolution immediately saw this and began, in their different ways, to court the crowd.

The crowd pleasers among the deputies had different talents. Mirabeau, who reigned supreme during the early months of the Revolution, delivered his blows against the *ancien regime* in a voice like thunder. Robespierre won the crowd with his ability to resonate to their deepest resentments and dress them up in sentimental rhetoric. Danton could summon up a fury which stirred the crowd to violent action. Desmoulins added a theatrical touch to his exhortations. Marat, the darling of the crowd, was in a class of his own. With his ferocious glare, his foul, unkempt appearance and his ability to rage tirelessly against the enemies of the people he was the perfect model of identification for the dispossessed inhabitants of the Paris slums. All these speakers had the intellectual, emotional and oratorical skills to mesmerize the crowd and turn what had been a leaderless group into a political instrument under their control.

Many of the crowd politicians were also deputies in the national legislature. But there were other demagogues for whom the crowd in the streets was their main, if not their only constituency. These extra-parliamentary demagogues held sway in the Paris Commune and in the Sections. The art of crowd control became more refined with every new operation. Each district had its separate militia bristling with arms; frequent meetings were held to keep emotions at fever pitch, and the tocsin was sounded to announce a special day of action whenever the leadership decided that the time had come to use the crowd like an army.

A crowd stripped of its symbolic coating and freed of the projections which it so readily attracts is a dynamic system made up of an aggregation of individuals who are in some form of communication with one another. Like any other group it has a boundary which separates it from its surroundings and an internal structure which gives it its distinctive character. And like other groups it is subject to the collective emotions, thoughts and fantasies which course through the communication network linking the individuals who constitute it.

However, it is the differences between a crowd and other types of group, rather than the similarities, which take us straight to the heart of the controversy which surrounds the crowd. Among groups which occupy a shared physical space a crowd is the largest, numbering anything between several hundred and several thousand people.

A crowd that assembles out in the open is a fluid entity, somewhat like an amoeba with pseudopodia, capable of becoming more concentrated or more attenuated according to its inner need and the nutrient medium of its immediate social context. It is a group with a highly permeable boundary, an unstable inner structure and a short lifespan. In comparison with more enduring groups it lacks organization, and this is where the controversy about crowds and leadership arises. Does the crowd generate its own leaders from within, or does a leader descend upon the crowd from without, as it were, and impose on it a structure which makes it a willing tool in the hands of its leader?

Because of its ephemeral nature, a crowd can only be held together by a unifying principle expressed through a highly visible and audible focus. The language of the crowd is stark, the symbolism bold. A speaker, performer or tableau must identify the mood of the crowd and give expression to that mood through speech and spectacle. These emotionally charged accoutrements of the crowd change it from an amorphous entity into a more differentiated organism, one with a head, so to speak, from which its collective thinking, mood and actions can be governed.

The disaffection of the Paris crowd encompassed feelings of rage and fear. These emotions were translated into acts which were given licence by the triumphant discovery that the boundary protecting the monarchy and the structures of the state could broken by sheer force of numbers. But in its formative stage this crowd was still a predominantly emotional group in search of a leader who could give it intellectual direction.

Politicians soon saw its potential to become a weapon in the decaying social context of the *ancien regime* and the crowd fell into the hands of men who steered it towards political power. Those who spearheaded the surge against the Bastille were reckless men whose muscle carried the day, but this early crowd was essentially unable to articulate their demands. It lacked a voice. The men and women who led the march to Versailles were fuelled by the triumph at their first conquest but they too were still far from having a coherent leadership.

When political demagogues eventually got in on the act and began to infuse the crowd with their rhetoric and claim ownership of the thoughts and feelings already in circulation, they soon discovered that they were riding a tiger. The crowd was insatiable, and it did not matter how eloquently some leaders argued on behalf of the crowd, there were always others who identified even more closely with the crowd's primitive needs and its lust for power. Some of these rival leaders had one foot inside the assembly of elected deputies, but there were others wilder still in their political outlook who identified so completely with the crowd that they caused even the more radical deputies to distance themselves uneasily from their demands.

In the five months since the convening of the National Assembly the Paris crowd had achieved three significant victories. The fall of the Bastille had shown that crowd power could be wielded successfully against military force, the march to Versailles had shown how easy it was to collapse the partitions which separated ordinary people from the royal family, and the king's abject display of revolutionary support in the presence of the crowd had proved that the monarchy could be subjugated to the will of the people.

After the crowd had brought its trophy back from Versailles there was a lull in the violence. The Assembly found a new home in the former riding stable of the Tuileries, and the Royal Family were housed safely, though in reduced circumstances, in the palace itself. It seemed as if the business of legislating for the new order could go ahead unhindered by violence. The Royalist elements in the National Assembly had more or less disappeared, having either fled the country or withdrawn from politics. Within the Assembly, however, the stage was set for a new polarization between radical and moderate revolutionaries, during which the Paris crowd did not disappear. It remained as an ominous latent force and its harbingers watched the proceedings in the Assembly with a baleful eye, ever ready to intrude if the call came.

Together with individual leaders who could speak the language of the crowd, there arose a more organized institutional leadership of the crowd. The Paris Commune, with responsibility for administering the city, established itself as a power base closest to the crowd in spirit, along with all the devices for mobilizing and marshalling the crowd at a moment's notice. The crowd could be summoned by the ringing of the tocsin and a bureaucratic machine soon came into being, comprising representatives of the Paris sections and local committees whose frequent meetings and frenzied propaganda meant that they could spirit up their constituents at short notice and send them into action.

This happened on 20th June 1792 when the crowd menaced and humiliated the king in the Tuileries and again three weeks later, when a second wave of crowd violence drove the royal family out of the Tuileries into the reluctant safekeeping of the assembly and signaled the overthrow of the monarchy. On this occasion, Louis, anxious as always to avoid bloodshed, instructed his Swiss Guard to offer no resistance and lay down their arms, whereupon they were slaughtered to a man. Three weeks later elements of the crowd, responding to the exhortations of the demagogues to root out the enemies of France, formed themselves into gangs and went on a killing spree which cost fourteen hundred lives.

What had once been a powerful but chaotic and ill-directed force had, with each successive wave of crowd action, become a more organized force, yielding its intrinsic power to a visible demagogic leadership. At first it was a question of who would lead this angry army of citizens. It soon became a question of who could control them. After the prison massacres of September 1792 the revolutionary leadership decided that the time had come to steal the crowd's thunder and assume responsibility for all further acts of violence. This meant giving the murder of political suspects a veneer of legality and representing it as a necessary ingredient of state policy.

The crowd during the Reign of Terror was a very different creature to the crowd of 1789. From having been a virtually leaderless group propelled by its own internal predatory urges it had evolved into a group directed by leaders who were on the outside but who had the power to point it in certain directions. It no longer flowed through the streets in search of victims but came instead to resemble a reserve army under orders to go into action at specific moments.

But there were still radical crowd leaders who would stop at nothing to destroy the distinction between crowd power and legislative authority. Among the men of the streets was a loosely knit group of radical democrats appropriately known as the *'enragés'*. Prominent among them were Jacques Roux, a vicar in one of the poorest parishes of Paris, and Jean Varlet, another cleric who attracted street crowds to his portable tribune. Both these demagogues ranted against the wealthy exploiters of the good, hard-working *sans-culottes*. Their message and that of other radicals who dominated the Paris Commune and the 'sections' into which the city had been divided was simple. The problems of the nation could only be solved by shedding the blood of all who were withholding bread from the mouths of honest, hard-working, starving citizens.

What finally brought these street demagogues into conflict with their friends inside the legislature was their decision to use the crowd as a means of intimidating those deputies who had taken a stand against them. This posed a threat to the inviolability of the elected representatives of the people. The radicals had their way on 2nd June 1793 when the crowd instigated a purge of the National Convention which resulted in the expulsion of a core of moderate deputies. But that was the crowd's last hurrah. From that point on it was the radical deputies who took over the acts of terrorism and murder for which the crowd had been responsible, and the crowd, from having been an instigator of bloodshed became its passive witness at the foot of the guillotine.

If we look at the way in which the Paris crowd has been written about by historians and politicians on both sides of the Left–Right divide, we can see that its symbolic aspect has continued to provoke conflict. Writers who were unsympathetic to the Revolution, Edmund Burke and Hippolyte Taine, for example, saw the worst in the Paris crowd and used intemperate language to describe it. Their writings were peppered with disparaging generalizations about the crowd ('rabble', 'brigands', 'swinish multitude' for example) and the terms 'mob' and 'crowd' were conflated and a sharp distinction was made between armies organized by the state and ill-organized masses of people.

On the other side of the divide, radical historians such as Jules Michelet and Alphonse Aulard referred to the Paris crowd grandly and simply as 'the people' and 'all of Paris' (*'tout Paris'*), and spoke reverently of the demagogues who roused them to action.

George Rudé, a twentieth-century historian who has tried to arrive at a more balanced perspective on the revolutionary crowd, has given a painstaking breakdown of the composition of the 'Conquerors of the Bastille' and shown that many were respectable artisans, hard-working people at the end of their tether and desperate for change.

From the time of the Paris Commune of 1871 until the outbreak of the First World War crowds, violence and revolution were strongly fused in the European mind. Advocates of revolution eulogized the crowd, while those who ruled the tottering empires and kingdoms of Europe used their waning military and political power to crush all signs of emergent crowd power.

With the rise of totalitarianism the crowd's tendency towards conformity was exploited by both fascists and communists. Leaders whose personalities resonated with the trauma and paranoia of the victims of war and revolution rose to prominence. These leaders realized that their power lay in their ability to hold up to the crowd the idea that the strength, power and pride which had been lost through war and revolution could be recovered with two provisos: First, that there must be complete and unconditional ('total') identification with the new leadership, (a single, god-like figure in the case of fascism, a monolithic, god-like group in the case of communism). The corollary of this idealization was the demonization of those presumed to have been responsible for the evils which had befallen the people.

The views of Hitler and Mussolini on the art of manipulating crowds were given intellectual substance by the theories of Gustav Le Bon, the most prominent among a new breed of reactionary, heavily politicized crowd psychologists. Le Bon's view of crowds was shaped by his traumatic experiences during the revolutionary violence of the 1871 Paris Commune, and he wrote relentlessly about the danger and insanity of crowd behaviour. For Le Bon the crowd was an animal-like mass which had to be regimented and controlled by leaders imposed on it from outside of it if its anarchistic proclivities were to be curbed.

Freud, perhaps through his own fear of anti-Semitic mobs, embraced Le Bon's negative view of the crowd, which he extended to a distrust of all groups. Thus he could write: 'A group is extraordinarily credulous and open to influence, it has no critical faculty and the improbable does not exist for it. It thinks in images, which call one another up by association (just as they arise with individuals in states of free imagination), and whose agreement with reality is never checked by any reasonable agency. The feelings of a group are always very simple and very exaggerated. So a group knows neither doubt nor uncertainty.'

This view was countered by the socialist perspective on groups put forward by a group of German sociologists, philosophers and psychologists including Theodore Adorno, Max Horkheimer and Herbert Marcuse. This group, who formed the Frankfurt School, harked back to the revolutionary principle that groups represented the will of the people and that the solidarity and comradeship inherent in groups could be harnessed in the service of the people as an antidote to total-itarianism.

Until the second half of the twentieth century the public view of the crowd remained essentially bipolar. Depending on one's political persuasion, the crowd symbolized either all that was worst in human nature or the opposite, the voice of the people's representatives on the march against tyranny. Then, in 1960 a seminal work by Elias Canetti ('Crowds and Power') challenged the prevailing dichotomous thinking about crowds and introduced a more nuanced scientific approach to the subject.

Talking about 'crowds' instead of 'the crowd', Canetti dispensed with the notion that crowds are a throwback to a more primitive stage in human evolution. The individual, therefore, should not regard himself as beyond barbarism simply because he is not part of a crowd. By the same token, the leader of a crowd is fundamentally no different from the crowd itself. The crowd is not ape to the leader's angel. For Canetti the crowd's core attribute is the feeling of equality which it confers on its members. People in a crowd experience a sense of merging with each other in a common bond. This kind of unification reduces the sense of fear in the face of external danger, but is terrifying to contemplate for those who are unable to submerge their individuality in the illusion of one-ness.

Those whose personalities impel them to seek power need crowds in order to consummate their power-lust. The omnipotent leader without a crowd at his disposal is impotent. Conversely, a leaderless crowd needs a leader to articulate the particular emotions which have brought it into existence. Canetti argues that it does not matter whether crowds seek out their leaders from inside or outside their own ranks. The important point is that power has its own chemistry which produces an attraction between the leader and the led. The illusion of unity which follows lasts only as long as the emotional needs of the whole group, including its leader, can be met.

With these insights it is possible to understand the story of the French revolutionary crowd as a series of attempted unions between power-hungry leaders and emotionally driven groups in search of a source of power.

CHAPTER SIX

Revolution *versus* Religion
God, Reason, and the God of Reason

'The man abused by fortune looks for bliss elsewhere. When he sees
the rich gratify all their tastes and indulge all their desires, while
his own requirements are restricted to the barest necessities,
he believes, and his consolation comes from his conviction,
that his bliss in the next world will be proportionate
to his privations in this one. Leave him with
this error of his.'
Danton, 30 November 1792

When the people have to endure suffering, Danton is saying, they dream of a better world. Let them dream on. This tolerant attitude towards religious belief was not shared by all the revolutionary leaders, although strangely enough Robespierre, for all his political monomania, never joined the anti-religious chorus. In the early days of the Revolution he had even argued the case for equal rights for Jews and Protestants, and a few years later he would invent his own brand of religious worship, while fiercely attacking the revolutionary campaign which paraded under the banner of de-Christianization. To Danton, religion was a harmless indulgence. To Robespierre, it was irrelevant unless it happened to get in the way of the march toward the Republic of Virtue, and that could only happen through the machinations of the Catholic Church, which the Revolution had already rendered impotent.

At the heart of the conflict over religion lay a battle for the mind. For centuries the Church had known that what people thought determined how they acted, and that if you could influence people's thoughts there was a fairly good chance that you could shape their actions in ways that suited you. People could be persuaded in different ways. They could be presented with stories which told of wonderful or terrible things that had once happened or would happen in the future, or they could be coerced into conformity by inflicting bodily pain in exquisitely varied ways. Cruel punishments, torture and killing would, of course, also serve as an example to the victims' families and fellow non-believers of what might happen if they strayed from the true path.

There were more subtle techniques, too, for influencing people's behaviour, which depended on the induction of altered states of consciousness. These techniques made the mind more suggestible, opening it up to the implantation of new ideas. The oldest civilizations had been aware that people could change the way they experienced the world if they gathered in groups and performed certain rhythmic actions in unison such as dancing or chanting.

We now know that these actions trigger resonances in the primitive parts of the brain which govern our emotions. The effect is to open up the gateway to the irrational mind and cause a shutdown of the intellectual powerhouse which normally overrides it. In other words, our ability to forge new perceptual and emotional connections is enhanced while our ability to reason and remember slips into the background. The stage is thereby set for the manufacture of illusions as replacement furniture for the mind, making us susceptible to new beliefs.

The effect of repetition, which forms the basis of ritual, is to bring the group closer together. Individual differences are submerged and melt into a sense of togetherness. The illusion is created that all are of the same mind, and with it comes the feeling of strength and power which reinforces the group's belief in its own survival in the face of danger. The earliest religious leaders realized this and saw the importance of stage-managing the settings in which people gathered to worship. They knew that rituals provided the framework, the emotional music, so to speak, for the intellectual and cognitive content of religious worship.

Today, of course, the use of repetitive techniques to stir the mind into states of heightened suggestibility is not only the prerogative of religious leaders. It colours every aspect of cultural life, including the political, artistic, sporting and economic. Families and communities are held in place by their participation in rituals which bind them to a central unifying principle. Whenever there is more than one central unifying principle, a tension arises between the principle of unity and the principle of diversity. Herein lies the drama and tragedy of human conflict. If the principle of unity prevails, the group achieves a strong sense of self from which sentiments such as nationalism and ethnic pride spring. But only up to a point. Beyond that point the group is set on a path to absolutism, totalitarianism and religious fundamentalism.

If, on the other hand, the principle of diversity prevails, the group experiences itself as composed of many selves and is set on a path to pluralism. But pluralism is a brittle state and it takes very little for a group to fracture into more than one self, each fragment developing into a new group and becoming alienated from the parent group. Our great task is to instil a culture of mutual identification into social groups with many selves, so that such groups can grow and allow differentiation without splitting into conflictual sub-groups.

Every religious and political group in the community establishes its own centre of power, a sort of factory where emotions and ideas are generated. These are then carried via messengers into the cultural matrix of the society. The process is analogous to the relationship between the nucleus of a cell, where information about the organism is held, and the organism as a whole, which reacts not only to the genetic information coming from the nucleus but to the information entering it from the environment which surrounds it. The cultural matrix is a vibrant network of communication, with the group trying to make sense of these two different sources of information.

The history of Europe from the rise of Christian power in the fourth century to the French Revolution is a sorry tale of persecution, massacre and warfare between different groups contesting for power. Each of these groups was convinced of its monopoly over truth and goodness and consumed by a passionate desire to become the central force dominating people's minds and bodies. In the apocalyptic thinking which marked man's early history the choice lay between annihilating one's enemy or being annihilated. Higher up on the scale of social evolution a slightly less barbaric choice appeared, the choice between dominating one's enemy or being dominated. Religion was to provide a third way: which was to convert the enemy into a friend, someone who shared one's beliefs. But this brought with it a whole new set of problems. How, after all, could one be sure of what was going on in the mind of one's newly created fellow believer? Would it not be better to drive out anyone about whom there was any doubt? At least excommunication, cruel though it was, was a more civilized way of getting rid of undesirable human beings than burning them or breaking their bodies.

Faced with such choices at an emotional level, man soon trained his intellectual mind in the belief that the struggle to survive was a struggle between the forces of good and evil. After that it became a simple matter to place every person and group in one or other of these two categories. Since the religious leaders of the day also happened to be the most educated, it fell to them (and they willingly took on the task) to show their communities how to divide the world between good and bad, according to the way people looked and behaved (and therefore thought). The ability to see people with fundamentally different views as being like oneself appeared relatively late in the evolution of the mind.

By the thirteenth century the conflict between secular and religious powers over which should take precedence had more or less resolved itself. There was a baleful agreement that no single body, and therefore no single leader, could command absolute power over both the spiritual and temporal domains of life. A deal was therefore struck in which the entity known as the human being was parcelled out between church and state, the former taking on custodianship of the person's soul, the latter laying claim to the body, which included the labour, property and land of the person. However, this agreement, which lay at the heart of the Feudal system, was no more than a truce. The struggle for power between religious and secular forces continued to burn like a fire that had not quite been extinguished, stirred up every now and then by an avaricious king or pope.

In the sixteenth century there was a further complication. The Church went through its own revolution in the form of the Reformation, giving rise to a new breed of ideologues who could see no reason why an elite group calling themselves priests were needed to mediate between the common people and their God, especially when their holy services had to be paid for in hard-earned cash. These new religious leaders railed against the corruption, hypocrisy and exploitation of the established church and soon established their own separate church. Now a fresh bloody conflict raged between those who wanted to purify Christianity and those who wanted to hang on to their power as God's agents on earth. It was a conflict that was to draw in kings, emperors and a host of tiny potentates who could not resist the temptation to increase their power by becoming champions of one or other side. After another hundred years of murder and devastation in the name of religion France emerged as the largest, most stable state in Europe. Louis XIV had done his bit for the Catholic cause by purging France of its Protestants, thereby rendering it a solidly Catholic country in thrall to a king who claimed to rule by Divine Right and a pope who claimed to be God's chief representative on earth.

In the minds of the revolutionaries, these two rulers, linked by the principle of divine right, became fused into a single symbol of oppression. The king and the aristocrats were the first and most visible targets of the Revolution, but the Church, known for centuries as the First Estate of the Realm, could not escape scrutiny for long, encased as it was in wealth and privilege and with its tight hold on the everyday lives of the people. The movement against the Church started slowly, but the rising tide of anger forced the people into an increasingly simplistic view of the Church as the fiendish ally of the nobility. Many of those who spearheaded the movement which was to develop into a full-blooded attack on Christianity were former priests who set about their task with all the zeal of 'born again' fanatics.

Rousseau's simplistic solution to the problems of society, which he put forward in *Du Contrat Social*, was that the individual should submerge all self-interest in the common interest of the group as a whole, or 'general will'. This was a magnificent vision of democracy, but quite how it was to be achieved in practice was not something that Rousseau the idealist bothered himself with. Montesquieu's more pragmatic starting point of complexity and diversity pointed towards a pluralistic solution to society's problems, but it was Rousseau who carried the day with starry-eyed revolutionaries like Robespierre, and the pluralistic solution was swept aside as an invitation to factionalism. In the religious context of the Revolution, there would be no room for organized religion and the laws of the state in the same society.

These philosophical and intellectual battles were running well before the outbreak of the Revolution. With the explosion of anger and excitement which announced the start of the Revolution they acquired a new significance. The structures in society which until then had provided the conduits for group emotions, the Church and the Monarchy, were now under attack by the very people whose emotional needs they were supposed to serve.

The dazzling splendour of the Royal family and the somewhat tarnished glitter of the aristocracy had once served to inspire awe in the common people at the existence of personages on whom divine authority had been conferred. At the beginning of the eighteenth century it was still held that the mere touch of a king could cure scrofula, a skin condition with swollen, ulcerated glands, probably tuberculous in nature. The Enlightenment provided the intellectual ammunition to attack such myths. The collusion of the Church and its patent self-interest in perpetuating these myths was also being exposed by the thinkers of the Enlightenment. One after another, the old icons came crashing down, but there was nothing to replace them except brand new social theories based on philosophical ideas which had never before been tried or tested in a political arena. Now was the moment to wipe the slate clean and make a new beginning for civilization.

Groups as well as individuals undergo that strange transformation of the mind described as being 'born again'. At a stroke, the past is renounced and a new way of life is passionately embraced. Those most prone to such a metamorphosis often carry with them a long history of brutalization through neglect or abuse. They steep themselves in addictions in order to wipe out the pain of the past and the despair of the present, and they struggle to control their murderous rage, which is directed both outwardly, at the real or symbolic perpetrators of their suffering, and inwardly, threatening to bring death upon themselves as the only solution to a life made unbearable by a sense of humiliation and failure.

The 'born again' transformation happens in a moment of crisis, sometimes experienced as a revelation of what was always there but was hidden. Suddenly a new solution appears to the conflict between committing murder or suicide. This is to start life all over again as if their past life had never existed. In the same way that those who have been traumatized shut themselves off from the painful memories of the trauma, those who have been 'born again' perform a mental operation which results in a massive bisection of their psyche. The world becomes sharply divided into the bad past and the good future. It is a wonderfully simple, crystal-clear solution which brooks no uncertainty.

Emotionally, the 'born again' person is in a state of constant fervour. At peak moments he may even become ecstatic. Most of the time he is resolute in his determination to purify himself of any relics from the past which might bring back painful experiences and contaminate his new world. His past life is consigned to a limbo in the unconscious mind and every conscious effort is made to construct a world which is exactly opposite to the hated world he has left behind. He feels rewarded and uplifted but knows he has to pay the price by expending constant energy to preserve his new world and keep the past at bay.

Such a person needs a group of like-minded people who will help him to avoid the noxious factors from the past. He often finds a home in a cult, sect or religion with a strong culture of emotional self-discipline, where passions can be diverted into carefully orchestrated and structured settings. He follows a doctrine of abstinence from behaviour which could activate thoughts, memories and feelings from the past. The group as a whole thrives on strict rules and rituals which harness the inescapable desires and rages of the human condition and channel them into carefully regulated avenues. There is little to fear from the temptation to fall back into old ways when one is cradled by observances and devotional activities to see one through all the days, months and years of one's new life. One's focus on the world narrows down intellectually to a concentration on often repeated texts. At the same time one's emotional field expands into experiences in which the boundaries separating the Self from the Other disappear. A new identity emerges, part of which may be the acquisition of a new name or title. The metaphor of a new age or a new dawn prevails.

The politicians of the Revolution looked around them at the ruins of the *ancien régime*. Within a year the institutions which had been standing for centuries had crumbled into dust. The fear of effective opposition by the king and the nobles had proved unfounded. The clergy, who in any case were a house divided, appealed in vain to the pope, whose thunderous condemnation of the Revolution failed to move the new leaders.

Into the political vacuum created by the disappearance of established institutions flowed a torrent of emotions, ideas and resolutions. On the evening of 4th August 1789 an astonishing scene took place in the National Assembly. One after another, nobles and prelates got up to renounce their rights and privileges, clearing away in one fell swoop most of the detritus which remained from the hated feudal system. The occasion had all the overtones of a religious frenzy, prompting one of the deputies to pass a note to the president urging him: 'Suspend the session. They have all gone quite mad!' In the cold light of the following day there were a few faint efforts to retract some of the self-abnegating measures, but the demolition had already happened. There could be no going back to the old order.

Many of the downtrodden people in France were seized with the spirit of hope when it looked as if the hated past was going to vanish and a new dawn was on the horizon. The mood of euphoria which overtook these people produced collective attitudes and beliefs resembling those of the 'born again' religious individual. As part of this rebirth everything had to change, first in the political domain and then in the religious domain. By 1793 the Monarchy had gone and a Republic had risen from its ashes. The Catholic Church had been dealt a body blow by the Civil Constitution of the Clergy, and the time was ripe to finish the job and bury the corpse. In the same way that attacks on the body politic by the most disaffected elements in society escalated into the political Terror, so too did the attacks on the Church escalate into the religious Terror. The two streams of the Terror coursed along as one.

No group, religious or secular, has a monopoly on any human emotion. The emotions which lift people up into a sense of wonderment or awe, or transport them into a feeling of communality with nature, life, one's fellow humans or some higher being, are regarded as the domain of spirituality, and this, traditionally has been the preserve of religion. But the conditions in which religious belief takes root and thrives are also met with in political groups. From the beginning the French Revolution had shown signs of religiosity. There was a feeling that what was happening would bind people together in communion, not with the Christian God, but with a state in which all would submit to the sovereign will of the people in return for the granting of everlasting human rights.

The changes to match the grand design had to be radical. There was much to be done in the political, military and economic spheres, but there were always a few leaders, the more histrionic, vehement and bloodthirsty ones, who made it a priority to expunge Christianity from the face of the Republic. The Gregorian calendar was thrown out and replaced by a Revolutionary calendar, the brainchild of a former actor called Fabre d'Églantine. The date on which the Republic was declared (22nd September 1792) became – retrospectively – day 1 of Year I. Religious holidays were abolished, months were given names with seasonal associations – *Vendémiaire, Brumaire and Frimaire* conjuring up autumn; *Nivôse, Pluviôse* and *Ventôse* winter; *Germinal, Florial* and *Prairial* spring; and *Messidor, Thermidor* and *Fructidor* summer. Each month was divided into three into ten-day periods bringing to an end the seven-day rhythm of the week with Sunday as the day of rest – an adjustment which, needless to say, proved highly unpopular with hard-working citizens of all political and religious persuasions.

The question was whether two belief systems, the one enshrined by centuries of tradition, the other newly born into a political vacuum, could co-exist within the same political entity – the French nation. As the Revolution gained momentum, the clash between the Catholic Church and the Revolution, which at first centred on privilege and the Church's identification with the monarchy, turned into a clash between Christianity and atheism.

To meet the people's emotional need for worship and celebration, the revolutionaries devised their own bizarre set of rituals which they enshrined as a Cult of Reason. All over France people were treated to strange spectacles: A donkey being led through the streets draped in the robes of a cardinal, young girls garlanded with flowers bobbing in front of a 'temple of philosophy' where the altar had once stood, groups of men and women in states of partial undress singing revolutionary songs and performing lewd dances to celebrate the Cult of Reason, and former priests standing up in evangelical vein to renounce their vows and declare themselves ready for marriage.

More horrible acts ensued in those provinces where counter-revolutionary activity was rife, and where many of the people were devout Catholics who deeply resented their faith being trampled on. Some of the deputies who had been sent out from Paris armed with unlimited powers to act in the name of the Convention instigated orgies of looting, confiscation of church property and desecration of churches. Priests, regardless of whether or not they had taken the oath of allegiance to the Republic, were driven out of office and many were imprisoned or executed. In Lyons, Joseph Fouché, a former priest and one of the most fervent de-Christianizers, herded three hundred people into a field, bombarded them with cannon fire and finished them off with bayonets. Another former priest, Joseph le Bon, travelled around the countryside with a group of so-called judges operating like a murder squad. Wherever they visited, the guillotine went into operation. The executions were treated like a festival, with spectators and victims forced to listen to a speech by le Bon followed by a band playing the revolutionary theme song, *Ça ira*.

In trying to understand the acts of the de-Christianizers we find ourselves entering murky waters. The hatred which they felt was partly a crusade of revenge. Many of the leaders of this movement were ex-priests who had been given licence by the Revolution to attack their symbolic parents. To them God was a punishing father with the Church a mother who had failed to protect them. Their obsessive attacks on Christianity remind us of the 'born again' mentality in reverse, a conversion away from religion instead of into it. Having led lives dominated by Christian austerity and self-denial, they suddenly entered a mind-set in which everything about Christianity was seen as evil.

These characters revelled in their sadistic acts, mocking the objects of their hatred, prolonging the agony of their victims and recounting with relish the details of the barbaric spectacles which they had orchestrated. Like so many people given power by a group whose ideology matches their own, they discovered the thrill of acting on their animal urges without fear of censure. One can almost see the outlines of a syndrome. The subject embraces a belief system which demands total commitment to a masochistic way of life. The reward for such self-inflicted suffering is a promise of happiness in the next world. But the subject's rage at his own suffering and powerlessness is overwhelming. He is then suddenly handed power by another group which promises him his reward, not in the next world but in this one. He breaks out of his masochistic shell and attacks those who remind him of his former self with all the madness and sadistic fury of a prisoner who suddenly finds himself liberated from the dungeon in which he has been incarcerated.

The fight to the death which finally ended the Reign of Terror came about because Robespierre had had enough of the de-Christianizers. A puritan at heart, he detested their bloodlust, foul-mouthed tirades, obscene rituals and atheistic preachings. The notion that death was no more than an eternal sleep, a favourite slogan of the de-Christianizers, offended him deeply, probably because it challenged his omnipotence and touched his fear of his own mortality. And he had an added reason for hating them. They were getting in the way of his own personal mission to bring the Republic back to religious worship.

Robespierre had never quite let go of his religious faith. In a rare moment of self-reflection he once mused that he had never been a very good Catholic, but neither had he ever embraced atheism. Now, during the escalating savagery known as the Great Terror, his messianic fervour impelled him towards a belief that religious and political belief was one and the same thing. Happiness and virtue would only come about if religion and politics merged into a single all-encompassing ideology. For this to happen the people had to return to a belief in God. But he could not bear the thought of a Catholic revival, which would mean the return of the hated priests and the re-estab-lishment of the Church. His compromise was to announce a new religion which would dispense with the trappings and rituals of Christian worship and offer the people a more introspective mode of communing with God (now renamed the Supreme Being) in keeping with the spirit of Rousseau. Somewhat at odds with these modest aspi-rations he then organized a grand festival to inaugurate his new religion.

It is an indication of Robespierre's power that he could drag the entire Convention to the Champ de Mars to participate in an absurd spectacle dubbed The Festival of the Supreme Being. Robespierre, draped in a tricolour sash and holding a bouquet, led the procession through a vast throng to the central tableau, where he made a tedious speech about the resurgence of Nature and the downfall of Tyrants. The theatrics of this extravaganza had been arranged by the painter David. The centrepiece of his tableau was a giant papier-mâché moun-tain on which the deputies seated themselves, facing a monstrous cardboard figure symbolizing atheism, to which Robespierre dramat-ically set fire. The idea was that the outer shell of the cardboard figure would shrivel up in the flames to reveal another cardboard statue inside it, a beautiful and dignified figure representing Wisdom, but the moment was slightly spoilt when the flames intended to consume Atheism also scorched Wisdom. Robespierre would not have failed to notice the sniggers of his fellow deputies, and it is easy to imagine the feelings of hatred burning within him alongside his precious tableau.

It would not be an exaggeration to say that Robespierre, under severe stress from the attacks being directed at him from all sides, had by now lost his grip on reality. The Festival of the Supreme Being lifted him into a state of religious ecstasy and brought into the foreground his grandiose delusion that he and the Revolution were as one. At the same time he could not escape the thought, which was rapidly becoming a fact, that his enemies were everywhere. He had recently been the target of two assassination attempts, and he was frequently mocked and challenged in the strident verbal exchanges which characterized the National Convention and the Committee of Public Safety. Those who attacked his new religion now became the worst sort of criminal in his fevered mind. They had struck at the very heart of his beliefs, and with his main adversary, Danton, out of the way, he concentrated all his energy on their destruction. His strategy was ingenious. Atheism, he declared, was an affront to religious freedom and an infringement of the people's rights. As such it was aristocratic in nature and a provocation to counter-revolution.

His enemies hit back with every weapon they could muster. They ridiculed his Cult of the Supreme Being, accusing him of wanting to be another pope. He was vilified as 'the dictator of truth' and 'the pontiff of the guillotine'. They could not fault the Incorruptible on his personal morals or his conduct of his financial affairs, but they did at last find a chink in his armour when it was discovered that he had signed a certificate of good citizenship for a deranged woman, Catherine Théot, who had extolled his virtues in the same breath as declaring that she was the Mother of God and that she would soon be giving birth to the Messiah. To the rabid de-Christianizers Robespierre, in signing the document, had lent himself to the forces of counter-revolution, especially since the old woman had gone about preaching her beliefs and had gathered a small following of pathetic individuals who could loosely be described as constituting a Christian cult. The bizarre case of the Mother of God was one more nail in Robespierre's coffin. It left him with a whiff of corruption and laid him open to further mockery over his messianic aspirations.

The holy citadel did not fall under the assault of the de-Christianizers. After the bloodbath which disposed of Robespierre and ended the Reign of Terror, those priests who had survived the Revolution came out of their hiding places, both inside and outside France, and began the task of restoring their vandalized churches and re-connecting with their congregations. It was business as usual, this time under the umbrella of counter-revolutionaries who closed down the Jacobin clubs with as much relish as the Jacobins had closed down the churches. It took a few more years for the Christian calendar to be reinstated but the arrival on the scene of Napoleon, the former Jacobin turned emperor who considered it expedient to have the pope on his side in his plans to conquer Europe, helped the process along. Once again the Catholic Church asserted its union with the forces of reaction and conservatism. But the genie of the Enlightenment could not be forced back into the bottle. Man now had new ways of thinking about himself, and the Revolution had given him new ideas on how he could govern himself. For all its durability, religion had lost some of its power.

The individual is usually outlived by the family into which he is born. The family in turn is outlived by the cultural group from which it springs, although the process can run to centuries. Larger groups, too, have a finite lifespan. States, empires and political conglomerates bound together by a common ideology rise, fall and vanish. The most enduring groups are those whose existence is based, not on the possession of land, wealth or physical might, or on their beliefs on how these should be distributed, but on their claim to be the custodians of the human spirit. Among these are the great monotheistic religions, which now co-exist uneasily with their rivals in the secular world, the offspring of the Enlightenment.

To this day there is a rift in society today between the pluralists and the fundamentalists, between those who believe that diversity is healthy and those who obey an imperative towards uniformity. In the depth of the social unconscious this is reflected in two different sets of fears and fantasies. For the pluralists there is no worse thought than sameness and the prospect of death by stagnation. They place their hope in the cross-fertilization of ideas and peoples. For the fundamentalists the nightmare fantasy is contamination. They thrive on fantasies of purity and perfection which can never be attained but must be constantly striven for by replicating an ideal image. They argue for the preservation of an unchanging core of society, a unity which can protect the people from themselves. Their view of man is that he is a lowly creature, prone to ungovernable urges, incapable of disciplining himself, having to be led and controlled by a higher force, either a human with god-like attributes or a god with human attributes. Fortunately the Orwellian scenario of total conformity to the whims of a central figure is an illusion which cracks under the weight of time. Within every society there are always hidden voices which speak out sooner or later to assert the freedom of the human spirit.

CHAPTER SEVEN

Heroes, Tyrants and Martyrs
The Assassination of Marat and the Murder of the Girondins

'I am the rage of the people.'
Marat

'This incredible calm, this entire dedication of self which shows no sign of remorse even in the presence of death itself, this complete tranquility and abnegation which in their way are sublime, are not natural. They can only be explained by that exaltation which is born of political fanaticism.'
Charlotte Corday's defence lawyer

'To this devoted band of men whose whole career was Justice and Virtue no one has dared to be contemptuous and history on every side has left them heroes.'
Hilaire Belloc, on the doomed Girondin deputies

By the summer of 1793 the leaders of the Revolution were in the grip of a paranoid dynamic which was propelling them towards an apocalyptic view of the world. Each of the leading factions saw themselves as the true custodians of the Revolution and regarded all who disagreed with them as the enemy. The mood underlying this mind-set was a mixture of fear and rage – fear of annihilation by France's enemies and rage at the betrayal of the people by the king and his followers.

The flush of exhilaration which suffused the national countenance in 1789 had gone. So too had the quiet optimism of 1790, when it looked as if all that was needed to bring the Revolution to fruition was for the National Assembly to roll up its sleeves and get on with the task of hewing a rock-solid constitution out of the Declaration of the Rights of Man and Citizen. However, the King's escape and recapture in June 1791 had destroyed the hopes of moderate-thinking revolutionaries that some form of constitutional monarchy could be cobbled together involving a tame king and his democratically elected subjects. The king's ignominious return to Paris had been greeted with stony hostility and the mood of the people changed overnight from one coloured by hope to one coloured by anger. By the time the much vaunted Constitution was finally produced, in September of that year, it was already dead in the water.

Having completed its task, the Constituent Assembly was obliged to dissolve, and its place was taken by an elected Legislative Assembly from which the original deputies of 1789 were excluded as a built-in safeguard against the temptations of abuse of power. However, the failure of the Legislative Assembly to solve the country's political, military and economic crisis and the collapse of the monarchy led to the call for a National Convention, which opened the door to radicals like Robespierre and Marat, who had been waiting in the wings to re-enter the stage of national power.

The conflict which underlay the French Revolution was as much a conflict of opposing mythologies as of political doctrines. On one side was the myth of power and privilege given by God to one ruler and passed down through ties of blood. Ranged against that was the myth of the tyrant who had enslaved a people, with heroes waiting to emerge who would liberate them. The drama and tragedy of the Revolution lay in the irreconcilable nature of these myths. One group invoked religion and tradition to support its mythology; the other invoked reason and the innate goodness of the people. The two groups for whom these myths formed the fabric of their collective identity could not co-exist in harmony. Neither group could identify with the other and each group saw in the other an alien and dangerous adversary.

Cultural myths are a composite of truth and fantasy forged over centuries in the powerhouse of the group's collective unconscious. Every culture has its own mythology with its cast of good and evil characters who enact cautionary tales for the benefit of future generations. It is through myth that the life and death struggles which belong to the human condition and the mysteries of nature are fleshed out and given meaning. The template for a drama in which good and evil are arrayed against each other is built into our minds from birth. As we mature we develop the capacity for reconciling good and bad within the same person or group but it only takes an experience of profound adversity for this mechanism to break down. When this occurs, attributions of badness fly out and attach themselves to a malign 'other' (individual or group) who must then be controlled or destroyed if the 'self' is to survive.

For the young mind in particular, myths reinforce a natural tendency to simplify and polarize. The world tends to be seen as an arena in which the forces of good and evil clash in mortal combat. On this battlefield there can be no compromise, no outcome other than victory, which means the assumption of power, or defeat, which means submission or death.

Young people are not only the passive recipients of myths, They actively shape them with their own fantasies which become superimposed on archetypal protagonists. The agents of good and evil are dressed in the costumes of the prevailing youth culture. Today's youngsters identify with lantern-jawed superheroes fighting metal-clad robotic tyrants from outer space. In eighteenth-century France, young Robespierre and his peers identified with heroes dressed in togas who fought to save the people from usurpers of power wearing robes of imperial purple. These heroes were men who led exemplary lives, espousing the virtues of self-discipline, austerity and loyalty to the state. They were picked out of the classical culture in which they were embedded and embraced as icons to be revered and emulated.

The future leaders of the Revolution were for the most part highly educated people. Many were lawyers, versed in philosophy, classics and the art of rhetoric. Some had literary pretensions and began their climb up the ladder of professional respectability by entering essay competitions on topics of social and political import. Camille Desmoulins, Jacques-Rene Hèbert and Jean-Paul Marat turned their literary skills towards journalism, albeit of the more vituperative variety. The young St Just, who was to become known as the Angel of Death, was a law graduate who announced himself to the literary world by writing a long, romantic, narrative poem with erotic overtones. Robespierre himself had tried his hand at poetry as a ticket of entry into an exclusive group of intellectual aesthetes, the Rosati, who held up the rose as an object of sensuous admiration and met regularly over a glass of wine to engage in learned discourses.

The seeds of their revolutionary mythology had been planted in the classroom. Although France was a solidly Catholic country, there had been a sea change in the educational system in the early 1760s when Louis XV succumbed to pressure from moderate Catholics and expelled the high church Jesuits. Responsibility for education passed into the hands of the Oratorians, a reformist group allied to the austere, civic-minded Jansenists. Many of the Oratorians were revolutionaries in spirit and they turned a blind eye to students who chose to dip into the seditious literature of the Enlightenment.

In addition to the dry religious studies which all good Catholics had
to digest, their students were raised on a diet of politics and legends
taken from the ancient Roman and Greek classics. France was a
country in which cruelty, self-aggrandizement and paternalism had
been amalgamated and institutionalized by the feudal system and it
was easy enough, when casting about for role models, to reach back
across the centuries to a remote past, to leapfrog over tyrannical kings
in the search for ideal leaders, to enter an idealized age and place in
which the state looked after the citizen in return for unquestioning
loyalty.

Rhetoric formed an essential part of their curriculum. Budding
young orators groomed themselves for a career in law by modelling
their speeches on the perorations of Cicero and striking mannered
poses learnt from actors in plays by Corneille and Racine. These
eloquent young men with hypertrophied intellects and stunted
emotional lives felt themselves to be victims of injustice and inequality,
and took on the identities of their ancient heroes with an enthusiasm
which more often than not clouded their judgment. The struggles of
their high-minded rebel heroes resonated with their perception of
France as a country in thrall to a tyrannical monarchy and furnished
them with messianic fantasies of rescuing the people through acts of
bravery and martyrdom.

There is a risk that idealized figures can steal into the personalities
of vulnerable young people and take them over, especially if there is
an emotional vacuum left by absent or negative parenting. Infatuation
with a hero fulfils unmet needs for self-esteem and gives the hero-
worshipper a sense of direction which real-life models have failed to
provide. More than that, the outlook and values of the hero-figure can
be swallowed holus-bolus in an act of incorporation which confuses
the true self with the imagined self of the adopted hero, creating a
Walter Mitty character with grandiose ideas about his role in human
affairs. With the risk of the Revolution collapsing and in an atmosphere of increasing paranoia, the embrace of classical mythology took
on the nature of a cult. The merging of identities was carried to absurd
lengths. There was a vogue for adopting the names of their heroes and
in some cases even dressing like them and sporting their hairstyles. For
these revolutionaries an alternative world sprang up in which Paris
became ancient Rome.

Camille Desmoulins, referring to the poor quarter of the Faubourg
St Antoine, in which the Cordelier's Club was situated, declaimed: 'I
never move about [it] without experiencing a religious feeling . . . and
on all its streets I read but one inscription, that of a Roman street, the
Via Sacra'.

The Roman Republic became their Holy City, an ideal state which had once existed in this world, and which could be re-built after the overthrow of Louis XVI. Louis became Tarquin the Proud, or sometimes Caligula, while Marie Antoinette was dubbed Messalina, the murderous and sexually rapacious wife of the Emperor Claudius.

In a world with no middle ground, assassination, filicide and cruel punishments were justified in the name of high ideals. Martyrdom was built into the character of the hero. There was no room for the Christian saints in the revolutionary martyrology. Catholicism and Royalty were seen as intertwined, and the places of the saints were taken by freedom fighters from the ranks of France's Gallic ancestors. Brutus, who murdered Julius Caesar to save the Roman republic from a descent into tyranny, provided the role-model for Charlotte Corday; and young revolutionaries sympathized with another earlier Brutus, leader of the revolt which led to the establishment of the Roman Republic, who executed his two sons for siding with the royal house of Tarquin.

After the king's flight the façade of revolutionary unity rapidly fell apart and the revolutionary movement crystallized into two bitterly antagonistic factions. Those who had been most closely identified with the king were now tainted by his 'betrayal' of the people and began to lose their slender grasp on the levers of power. This group of deputies, moderate in the sense of their belief in a constitutional monarchy but bellicose in their call for a war against France's external enemies, suddenly found the ground cut from under their feet.

Known as the Girondins, because many of them came from the region of the Gironde, they found themselves locked in a life and death struggle with the radical deputies, the Montagnards, or Men of the Mountain, so called because they occupied the highest tiers of seating in the National Convention, to the left of the presidential tribune. These men had the backing of the Paris Commune whose leaders could call a mob into action at the ringing of the tocsin.

The nation's survival now seemed to rest on the people's ability to destroy all its enemies, both inside and outside France's boundaries. Throughout the spring and summer of 1793 the government of France was waging a brutal civil war as well as the war on her frontiers. The Girondins found themselves lumped together with the traitor-king in an ever enlarging category of enemies which included priests who had refused to take the oath of loyalty to the constitution, foreigners, citizens judged to be lukewarm in their commitment, peasants who resented being pulled away from their land to fight for a cause which had trampled over their beloved church, defeated army generals and merchants and traders accused of hoarding or corruption.

The Girondins opposed the view of the Mountain that the compass of democracy should extend beyond the elected deputies to include the common people. Both factions waged a highly personal war, fielding their best orators like gladiators in single combat. The wild accusations, threats and appeals to the people which flew back and forth (amply laced, of course, with classical allusions) played to an audience both inside and outside the legislature. Leading Girondins delivered ringing denunciations of Robespierre and Marat which enraged the people of Paris.

The idealistic appeals of the Girondins for justice and an end to violence fell on stony ground. Their mistake, and also their tragedy, was that they failed to address the rage of the people of Paris, who continued to face food shortages and economic hardship and who had no time for political sermons couched in overblown prose. The Girondins' furious and self-righteous attacks on Robespierre and Marat were experienced as attacks upon the people themselves. The Men of the Mountain, on the other hand, could articulate the rage of the people. Robespierre could give it ideological body while Marat could sound its raucous voice in the chamber of the National Convention and point a finger at the deputies against whom it should be directed.

In the dream world which they inhabited, the Girondins believed that their status as elected representatives of the people would protect them from the violence which they denounced. They believed that the National Convention was a sanctuary of free speech, and that the deputies who sat there were inviolate. In the end they were brought down by the concerted efforts of those within the Convention, including Marat, Robespierre and even Danton, a potential ally whose overtures they had spurned and whom they had antagonized by their vitriolic assaults on his integrity, and on those outside its walls, the *sans-culottes* who controlled the streets and took their cue from the Paris Commune. On 2nd June 1793 a crowd of some eighty thousand armed *sans-culottes* surrounded the Convention and demanded the arrest of the leading Girondins.

In the midst of this dramatic stand-off some two hundred deputies walked out of the Convention chamber, ostensibly to mingle with their fellow citizens in order to show that they were at one with the people, but also to look for a way out of what had become a frighteningly menacing situation. They encountered a wall of sans-culottes in an ugly mood, leaving them no choice but to troop disconsolately back to their benches. Under the feeble guidance of the president of the day, Hérault de Séchelles, the Convention capitulated and voted for the expulsion of twenty-nine Girondin deputies, who were led off into house arrest.

Overnight the Girondins became a persecuted political minority. Some escaped to their native provinces from where they continued their fight against the radicals of Paris. Others were hunted down or committed suicide. Twenty-two of the twenty-nine who had been expelled were subjected to a mass trial which was cut short in order to stifle the anticipated outpouring of persuasive oratory which would prove an embarrassment to their judges. All were guillotined, including one who had stabbed himself to death on hearing the sentence.

Among the leading figures who perished were Jacques-Pierre Brissot, leader of the pro-war faction in the Legislative Assembly and Pierre Vergniaud, whose inspired oratory had stirred passions of a re-awakened national glory at a time when France was beginning to feel that it had lost contact with its grand heritage. Both Brissot and Vergniaud had held an obsessive hatred of Robespierre which was cordially reciprocated. But even Robespierre had been reluctant to herd the Girondins towards the guillotine and had aborted a call for the execution of seventy-one deputies who had stood up in support of the expelled Girondins. Perhaps he had seen the writing on the wall in this violation of parliamentary sanctity and was beginning to draw new lines of battle to protect his shrinking inner circle.

As with so many of the groups which flowered and were destroyed during the Revolution, the Girondins became invested with divided political symbolism. They came to be seen by leftist politicians as the prototypes of a soft-bellied bourgeois conservatism and petty nationalism, a group who appealed to the worst instincts of the old regime while parading a new-found brand of social liberty which took no account of the economic plight of ordinary workers. Liberal politicians, on the other hand, admired them as the embodiment of the true revolutionary spirit, victims of a faction whose perversion of the Revolution had turned France back towards tyranny and down the path of violence and terror. It was the old story of heroes and monsters glaring at each other without seeing their own reflections in their adversaries.

Charlotte Corday, the young woman who was to make her mark on the history of the Revolution with a single thrust of a kitchen knife, lived in the ancient town of Caen in Normandy, where many Girondins had fled after the *coup* which had driven them out of the Convention.

Before moving to Caen she had lived a rural life, the daughter of an impoverished, embittered farm owner of noble extraction who played little part in his daughter's upbringing other than to arrange for her to be boarded at a convent at the age of fifteen following the death of her mother. The abbess of the convent remembered Charlotte as a clear-headed girl, fond of arguing against the received wisdom and singularly unsuited to the obedience required for a religious life. The formative influence in her life was an uncle, a retired abbot, with whom she cloistered herself for hours at a time, poring over the writings of Tacitus, Plutarch, Rousseau and her great-uncle, the playwright Corneille. Having been intellectually and emotionally groomed for the Revolution, Charlotte wholeheartedly embraced the idealistic spirit which greeted its advent. However she was traumatized by her exposure to gruesome acts perpetrated by mobs in her region and she withdrew into herself, shaken and confused. Her mind cleared when the Girondins emerged as the torch-bearers of revolutionary ideals and the opponents of mob violence.

Charlotte identified passionately with the Girondins, whose language she understood, and she reviled the Montagnards, who, in her mind, stood for violence and terror. As far as she was concerned, the underlying political issues were subordinate to the clash between the ideal and the demonic, the former represented by civilized discourse, the latter by primeval brutality. Watching the dramatic events in Paris from afar and sharing in the attempts by the Girondins in Caen to rally support and carry on the fight, she decided that the most evil figure among the detested Montagnards was Marat, the person who had been chiefly responsible for the expulsion of the Girondin deputies from the National Convention. In her fevered imagination, Marat had ripped out the heart of the French people, and the solution which crystallized in her mind was to avenge this act by killing him. Only then, she believed, could peace be restored and France saved.

Her decision was only arrived at after an agonized period of inner conflict. She had written again and again on pieces of paper, 'Shall I? Shall I not?' and she had even embroidered these questions on a piece of material before making up her mind. Once the decision had been taken, however, she passed into a dissociated state of mind in which all her powers of concentration were focused on making the necessary plans to stalk her intended victim while the rest of the world receded into an unreal background.

Without disclosing her intentions to anybody, she persuaded one of Girondins to give her letter of introduction to a sympathetic deputy in Paris, ostensibly to conduct some business on behalf of a mutual friend, but really to give her a ticket of entry into the National Convention. In return for this favour she offered to act as a courier for any papers he might want delivered to his friend.

She then set about methodically putting her affairs in order, tidying her house, returning borrowed books and distributing some of her personal possessions – earrings, needlework, a book of lace designs – to friends, with remarks which puzzled them at the time, that she would have no further need of those items. She spent the few days before her departure saying goodbye to lifelong friends. A woman who lived in the village where her aunt had a farm observed that though her person was present, 'her spirit was elsewhere'. At home with her aunt she gave way to spasms of weeping, exclaiming on one occasion, 'Marat will never rule France!'

She told her aunt that she was going to visit her father in his home town of Argentan, while at the same time she wrote to her father: 'I am leaving without seeing you because I am too full of grief. I am going to England. I don't believe that that one can be happy or calm in France at this time . . . Heaven has refused us the happiness of living together as it has denied us so many other blessings. Perhaps it will be clement toward our country. Adieu, my dear father. Embrace my dear sister for me and do not forget me.'

Charlotte Corday's 'Address to the French People', composed in her hotel room the night before the deed, gives a good insight into the mind of a person set on the road to martyrdom. 'How long, O unhappy Frenchmen', she began, 'are you to suffer this trouble and disunion? Too long have scheming men and scoundrels put their ambition ahead of public interest. Why, unhappy victim of these disturbances, do you tear out your heart and destroy yourself to establish this tyranny on the ruins of desolated France? . . . Oh, my country! Your misfortunes break my heart; I can only offer you my life, and I thank heaven that I have the freedom to dispose of it.'

She went on to declare that she did not consider her act to be either murder or a crime. Marat, she wrote, had been condemned by the universe and his bloody deeds had placed him outside the law. Her concluding statement was that her relatives and friends were innocent of any knowledge of her enterprise. This was the testament, which, together with her baptismal certificate, was found pinned to her bodice when she was apprehended.

In Paris, a casual conversation with a waiter gave her the information that Marat had been too ill recently to attend the Convention.

This put paid to her cherished idea of accosting him in the hall of the Convention and stabbing him to death in the manner of a Brutus meting out the people's justice to the tyrant Caesar. Undeterred, she fell back on another plan, which was to confront the monster in his den and gain an audience with him on the pretext of having information about plots being hatched by his enemies in the provinces.

Early on the morning of Saturday, 13th July 1793, she made her way to the market place at the Palais Royale, where she bought an ebony-handled kitchen knife with a six-inch blade in a green cardboard sheath. She slipped the knife into the pocket of her dress, entered a cab and asked the driver to take her to the residence of Marat, not having the faintest idea herself where he lived. The driver himself had no idea either, but after consulting with his fellow cabbies he delivered his passenger to her destination, a first-floor apartment in the rue des Cordeliers where Marat lived with his mistress Simonne Evrard, her sister Catherine and his own sister, Albertine. Charlotte was directed up a flight of stone stairs to the door, which was opened by Catherine Evrard who, after sizing up the visitor, brusquely informed her that Marat was too ill to see anybody. A moment later she was joined by Simonne, who cut short Charlotte's explanation and closed the door on her.

Once again undeterred, Charlotte returned to her hotel where she wrote Marat a short note: 'I come from Caen. Your love for your country should make you curious to know the plots which are afoot there.' With more than a hint of irony she added, 'I will put you in a condition to render great service to France.' She signed her name, gave the address of her hotel and asked for the note to be delivered. Meantime, she had recourse to another expedient. Summoning a hairdresser to give her a more stylish hairdo, changing her dress and adorning her hat with striking green feathers, this tall, beautiful woman who had never before resorted to coquettish ploys, set out again on her mission, this time hoping to catch the eye of Marat for just long enough to stimulate his male interest and curiosity. Having waited in vain for a response to her earlier note, she had written another note to have in readiness which said, ' . . . My great unhappiness gives me a right to your protection.' She lodged the sheathed knife in her bodice, put on a pair of white gloves, and carrying a green paper fan which matched the feathers in her hat, set out once again for Marat's apartment.

It was early evening, a busy time in the Marat apartment, which also served as a distribution point for Marat's newspaper. Charlotte took advantage of the simultaneous arrival at the apartment of two men on newspaper business to step over the threshold and begin a heated argument with the women of the household, who once again tried to bar her way. This time, however, Marat, who could overhear the woman visitor repeatedly asking if he had received her letter, ordered that she should be admitted. He had in fact read her letter, his curiosity had been aroused and he was intensely interested in what she had to say about his enemies in Caen.

Marat sat in his bathtub, a shoe-shaped copper-backed contraption which shielded him to well above his waist. A long board, on which stood an ink bottle, a quill and some paper, lay across the front of the tub, serving as a sort of writing desk. Marat invited his unusual-looking visitor to sit on a stool next to him and began scratching away with his quill as soon as he heard the names of some well-known Girondins. Having lulled him with this apparently authentic recital of names Charlotte suddenly rose from her stool, drew the knife from its sheath and plunged it into his chest, narrowly missing his rib-cage and puncturing his aorta. Marat could do no more than utter a loud cry which was heard throughout the apartment: '*À moi, moi cher amie; à moi!*' (Help, dear friend; help!)

As Marat's life ebbed away and with pandemonium breaking out, Charlotte Corday walked calmly towards the door of the apartment. One of Marat's employees testified what happened next: 'The monster had reached the antechamber. I seized a chair to stop her, so with a great blow of the chair I floored her. The creature struggled to rise,' continued this would-be hero. 'Defying her strength, I seized this monster by her two breasts, knocked her down again and struck at her.'

The National Guard and Police soon took over. Against a background of distraught cries and screams the district police commissioner began his preliminary examination, noting that 'the prisoner testified that she wished to sacrifice her life for her country'. 'She has every grace, she is tall and of superb bearing', observed one of her unsavoury interrogators, an ex-monk from the Committee of General Security. Charlotte maintained her composure throughout this ordeal. As she was being hustled through the surging crowd she quietly remarked, 'I have done my duty. Now let others do theirs.'

Everyone who saw her was impressed by her air of serene detachment. Only a few times did she show signs of being angry or upset. When the prosecutor put to her that there might have been other occasions on which she had done people to death she was outraged. 'They take me for a common assassin!' she exclaimed.

She was shocked, however, when she realized that she had compromised a fellow Girondin by keeping company with him the day before the assassination, thereby implicating him as a co-conspirator. And she had another moment of visible distress and had to turn her face away when she noticed the sobs of Marat's widow. Later, in prison, she wrote: 'The crying of certain women upset me. But if one saves one's country one must not think of the price that has to be paid.' She retained her composure to the end, firmly convinced that she had 'rid the world of a monster and saved ten thousand lives'.

The trial ran its predictable course in the presence of a hushed crowd. To the suggestion that others must have been complicit in her crime, she retorted: 'You do not understand the human heart. It is far easier to execute a plan such as this when one is inspired by one's own hatred than when one is inspired by the hatred of others.'

In this reply lies the key to an understanding of Charlotte Corday's mentality and that of many before and after her who have sought death in martyrdom. The mind of the martyr holds the thought that self-sacrifice is necessary for the survival of others. This idea, noble in one sense, murderous in another, is central to the motivation of the martyr. The 'self' is harmed, even destroyed, so that the 'other' can survive. But martyrdom also thrives on hatred, whether or not this is consciously acknowledged. Martyrdom, at least of the self-appointed sort, is, in its most extreme manifestation, an act of suicide. Death is embraced as a preferable option to life under unbearable circumstances, and the act of killing oneself is governed by a hatred of the most intense kind, directed at whoever is perceived as being responsible for the plight of the martyr.

Ironically, Charlotte Corday and Marat, both isolated figures in their own way, had something in common. Both were idealists and murderers, fuelled by dreams of a perfect society and hatred of those who stood in the way of its advent. For Charlotte Corday, the romantic dreamer, the solution was simple. The path to the promised land could be cleared by killing the monster who had wounded her beloved France and was now threatening to destroy it. Her mind was more like that of a stalker, a person in love who has been deeply injured. For Marat, whose fulminating hatred made him see enemies everywhere, the monster was a many-headed hydra, and the path to his promised land could only be cleared by slicing off the heads of the thousands of greedy and selfish tormentors of the nameless poor with whom he identified. His was more the mind of a genocidal killer, a political fundamentalist for whom the solution to the problem of opposition lay in the elimination of all who would not accept the truth as revealed by his version of the Revolution.

Martyrdom is not only a self-appointed role. It is a role conferred by the group on those who are seen to have sacrificed themselves for the sake of the group. Without this complementary acknowledgement of self-sacrifice, the would-be martyr leaves behind only a feeling of futility and resentment. Charlotte Corday operating secretly and alone, literally hugging her blueprint for the nation's happiness to her bosom, passed from the scene with none of the posthumously awarded trappings of martyrdom. If anything, the Girondins with whom she so passionately identified saw her sacrificial act as exacerbating the already fervid hostility against them without achieving any political gain. One of them, Vergniaud, remarked grimly: 'She has killed us, but she has taught us how to die.' Another, Guadet, observed dryly that if only she had consulted them first they might have pointed her towards Robespierre, with a significantly greater likelihood of influencing the course of events.

Unlike Charlotte Corday, who nursed messianic fantasies and longed for her own martyrdom, Jean Paul Marat saw himself as still having much work to do in the disposal of his enemies and was of no mind just yet to volunteer for death. A man of intense ambition (of which, unlike Robespierre, he made no secret), he had once served as physician to the Count of Artois, brother of Louis XVI and had seen himself as a scientist and inventor whose discoveries in the fields of electricity, optics and aeronautics should have been recognized by the foremost scientific academies in Europe. His rejection by those august bodies turned his grandiosity into paranoid rage, which found expression in revolutionary journalism and a crowd-pleasing oratory of a vituperative kind which made even his Montagnard associates uneasy.

Marat's monster-like image was reinforced by his affectedly dishevelled appearance, aggressive social manner and harsh, grating voice, all of which gave rise to no end of insulting epithets likening him to lower life forms from the hyena to the toad. It was known that he had taken refuge in a dank cellar while on the run from the authorities, and this, coupled with the fact that he had contracted a particularly nasty skin condition, contributed further to the general air of repulsiveness which emanated from him. He sat alone, even on the benches of the National Convention. If the triumvirate of Robespierre, Danton and Marat which revolutionary mythology has handed down to us can be allocated to the roles of The Good, The Bad and The Ugly, there may still be arguments over which of Robespierre and Danton would occupy the roles of The Good and The Bad. Marat, however, indisputably occupies the role of The Ugly.

After his death, Marat, hero of the people, was promoted to instant martyrdom by his grief-stricken followers, with the sanctimonious help of the Convention. Robespierre, however, held himself conspicuously aloof from all the theatrics surrounding the death. He had been outflanked on the Left by this champion of the people, and now his own privately cherished role of martyr had been usurped.

Marat's funeral procession, stage-managed by the painter Jacques Louis David, turned into a macabre circus. The most potent symbol of his martyrdom, his eviscerated heart, lay in an urn (it would later be hoisted in a casket to the ceiling of the pantheon). There was no shortage of other relics, either – the bloodstained shirt on a pike, a chalice allegedly containing Marat's blood and even the bathtub, carried by four women. Overnight Marat had become a secular saint, with busts of him appearing all over France, replacing those of the Christian saints. David's painting of the dead Marat lying in Christ-like repose in his bath has become one of the enduring icons of the revolution, a reminder of the central role played by the visual arts in the reinforcement of myths.

The story of Marat and Charlotte Corday, a tragic duo united only by hatred and death, provides a good illustration of the reciprocal relationship between martyrs and monsters, saints and devils, good and evil. Both believed that they were rendering a service to their people by performing their murderous acts. Both invited death by throwing themselves into the fight against what they saw as the forces of evil. Martyrs are not scapegoats. The latter are seized by the enemy as representatives of an alien 'other' group, whether they are in a state of active resistance or passive helplessness. Martyrs step forward with acts of defiance or counter-attack against the odds in a spirit of rescue and in the belief that there is a future greater than themselves which lies beyond death.

But it is left to the group which survives the act of martyrdom to endorse the role of martyr or disown it. Marat's tenure of martyrdom lasted less than eighteen months. In the aftermath of the Terror a nervous Convention decreed that his heart should be lowered from the ceiling of the pantheon on the grounds that no one should be declared a saint for at least ten years after their death. Charlotte Corday's martyrdom was absorbed into that of her beloved Girondins, and they in turn have been reduced by posterity to a political faction with high principles but poor judgment, a flamboyant, colourful group of politicians who spoke well but fought badly.

CHAPTER EIGHT

The Reign of Terror
A Study in Group Paranoia

'Let us be terrible so that we can prevent the People from being terrible.'
Danton

'[The Reign of Terror was] not the reign of people who inspire terror,
but of people who are themselves terrified.'
Engel, in a letter to Marx

'In time we hate that which we often fear.'
Charmian in *Antony and Cleopatra* (1.3), Shakespeare

The Reign of Terror has been likened to a carbuncle on the smooth surface of the Revolution. The Terror was not, however, an epiphenomenon or an aberration from the true course of the Revolution. To epitomize it as such would be to perpetuate the split in thinking which casts the Terror as 'bad' and the Revolution as 'good'. Both the Terror and the Enlightenment were elements of the same dynamic process.

The roots of the Terror ran as deeply in society as those from which the Revolution in its noblest manifestations sprang and were intertwined with each other before they saw the light of day as separate branches of the same tree. Many of those who promulgated the Terror, such as Robespierre and Danton, had been promoting enlightened legislation from the earliest days of the Revolution and found themselves torn apart by the uncontrollable violence which heralded the Terror and which was tearing the country apart.

At the start of the Revolution the current of violence flowed alongside that of euphoria. As the realistic obstacles in the way of the revolutionary goals emerged, the euphoria ebbed and the violence became a torrent. The first grand vision of the Revolution had been a co-operative understanding between the monarchy and the sovereign people. It was a dream of harmony between two god-like parental figures out of whose union a child would be born, a society in which all would be free and equal.

For a while it had seemed as if the efforts to join the monarch in holy matrimony to his sovereign people might work. The deputies of the Constituent Assembly had laboured to cobble together a constitution which would reflect the happy union and serve as a birth certificate for their newborn child. Eventually they produced the document, but by that time the mood of the country had changed, and the Legislative Assembly which took over from the Constituent Assembly was left with a mutually hostile couple and a sickly infant with an uncertain identity.

Neither the king nor the revolutionaries had been willing to make this symbolic union work. The king's flight to Varennes in June 1791 had confirmed the fears about his betrayal of the revolutionary cause. A month later, a huge gathering to support a petition for the abolition of the monarchy was fired on by the National Guard, with some fifty persons killed or wounded, in what became known as the Massacre of the Champ de Mars. Violence was in the ascendant, and the mood of optimism was being eclipsed by a mood of anger and a grim determination to protect the Revolution at all costs, which included getting rid of the king. The precariously unified revolutionary movement split open along a crack dividing those who still held out some hope for salvaging the wreck of the constitutional monarchy from those who wanted a republic.

The Reign of Terror arose in the context of a vicious cycle. The violence with which the Revolution announced itself provoked counter-violence from those in power and this provoked retaliation. In the early phases of the Revolution, it was clear who the enemy was, but once the *ancien regime* had been overthrown and the pyramid of power had been stood on its head, no one was quite sure who would be the next enemy. Counter-violence, or 'terror' exercised by those newly in power, began to have appeal not only as a legitimate way of getting rid of one's remaining enemies but as a sop to the people who still saw no improvement in their lot and continued to feel threatened by every turn of events.

While this was happening, both the individual and group leadership of the Revolution changed. New men, with greater capabilities for managing the violence, assumed positions of power. Violence does not brook ambivalence. It delivers axe-like blows into the unity of large groups and drives people to seek shelter in smaller groups led by people under whose leadership they feel safer. Ideas as a unifying principle become less important than personalities deemed strong enough to provide protection.

Danton was ambivalent about the Terror. So to a lesser extent was Robespierre. But there were other ruthless men who seized the opportunity to exercise power as the Terror reached its height, men who had neither the compassion of Danton nor the idealistic misgivings of Robespierre. These men were quick to see that in a world peopled by enemies (real or imaginary) survival lay with those who could wield the greater power. In the war of words which the Revolution had become, those who could proclaim the spirit of the Revolution more effectively and denounce their enemies more swiftly would carry the day.

During the culmination of the Reign of Terror, the increasingly broad definitions of who constituted an enemy of the Revolution and the impossibly narrow concept of revolutionary goodness brought these extremists into a collision course with moderate revolutionaries and ultimately with Robespierre himself, who, in an ironic denouement, was made to appear at once both moderate and treasonous in accusations framed in the terms which he himself had invented to denounce enemies of the Revolution.

Many of the leading revolutionaries were idealists who were carried away by their own rhetoric. They were prey to the same primitive emotions as those which governed the citizens on whose behalf they were fighting, people who were quick to resort to violence and bloodshed as a way of alleviating their own fear and rage. This placed the idealists in a conflict. If they took measures against popularly inspired violence they ran the risk of being branded as tyrants no better than those whom they had displaced. On the other hand, if they sanctioned such violence they were effectively placing power in the hands of its perpetrators, weakening their own hold on power and delaying the advent of the society for which they were so zealously working. Their solution, therefore, was to twist their rhetoric into a shape which would soothe the savage breasts of their followers by painting a rosy vision of the future while at the same time deflecting rage over past and present suffering onto named 'others'.

As well as the emotions associated with the need to survive, there were those emotions associated with the anticipation of a better life, the prospect of a new dawn after the long night of Bourbon rule. The first revolutionary explosion was greeted with a fervour bordering on religious ecstasy, a euphoric mood captured in Wordsworth's memorable line: 'Bliss was it in that age to be alive, but to be young was very heaven.'

The revolutionary leaders were swept along in the swirl of these contradictory emotional currents. The only way they could hang on to power was to claim ownership of both these sets of emotion, infuse them with their own thoughts and ideas, and present them to the people as a pathway out of chaos and confusion.

The leaders who emerged were therefore those who were best able to perform this almost impossible double act. In one breath they had to justify the violence which sprang from rage and fear and sustain the mood of optimism which sprang from hope. They were caught up in a battle to gain mastery over a situation which felt increasingly out of control, in which they had to contrive a language which would reconcile their vision of a new world with the destruction of the old one.

In this frenetic atmosphere it was impossible to achieve a unity of purpose. During the first eighteen months of the Revolution voices of compromise could still be heard. Mirabeau, for all his thunderous oratory, worked furiously behind the scenes to bring the royal family to their senses; Lafayette, hero of the American War of Independence, galloped to and fro as an intermediary between the king and the people; Sieyès, powerful advocate of the rights of the people, wanted nothing more than a constitutionally enshrined accommodation between nation and monarchy. But these voices of moderation were drowned by the onrush of rage which welled up from the most disaffected elements of the nation.

The revolutionaries were trapped in an ideological paradox of their own making. By their own determination there could be no such thing as loyal opposition to the Revolution. Therefore there could be no formal political parties. Accordingly there was no legitimate outlet for organized disagreement among the representatives of the people. Any such tendency was seen as an attack on the principle of unified sovereignty, given the abusive label of 'factionalism' and treated as a crime against the Revolution itself.

The different factions therefore came to be identified not by any specific ideology but by the name of the dominant figure in the legislature who best articulated his case for being the true custodian of revolutionary values. It was the political equivalent of a beauty contest, a sort of 'truth' contest, in which the price of failure was to be in error and therefore pronounced an enemy of the Revolution.

In this atmosphere of political chaos and life-threatening aggression there could be no clear direction of policy, and the best hope of safety for the people's representatives seemed to lie in identifying with a chosen dominant figure rather than an ideology, forming an attachment to a person in the flesh who could protect you instead of an abstraction, an ideology which could be redefined overnight as counter-revolutionary.

The leaders of these smaller factions promptly began to savage one another, in grim fulfilment of Vergniaud's prophecy that the Revolution would devour its own children. In the nightmare struggle for survival the Robespierrists occupied the radical core, the Dantonists took on the mantle of 'moderatism' after the destruction of the Girondins, and the Hèbertists, the militant atheists of the Revolution, waged an unrelenting war, not only against the Christian church but against anyone to the left or right who challenged their views. Only Marat, who was assassinated in July 1793, did not survive long enough to acquire a factional identity or gather his own personal following among the deputies. One after another the radical leaders and their islands of followers were destroyed until the revolutionary movement itself disappeared beneath the waves.

The new leaders were those who could articulate the undiluted rage of the people. For them, the vision of the new world was less important than the destruction of the old one. In the minds of these emerging leaders the aims of the Revolution could only be fulfilled by the elimination of the people responsible for the perpetuation of their suffering. This entailed a wide sweep of alleged perpetrators labelled, truly or falsely, as royalists, aristocrats, priests who had refused to take the oath of loyalty to the state, profiteers, and hoarders.

Even within the category of radical leadership there was a spectrum ranging from characters like Danton, whose gigantic presence straddled both moderate and extremist camps; to the reluctant Robespierre, who tortured the language of his rhetoric into a vain attempt to reconcile the contradictions between revolutionary idealism and the necessity of managing the rising torrent of violence; to the embittered Marat who ranted both in speech and print against any compromise with so-called moderatism; to the bloodthirsty Hébert, whose frenzied and obscene outpourings blurred all distinctions between major and minor transgressors and who, like a Dalek, called for the extermination of all who came within his sights.

Each of these fanatical leaders carried a semblance of political respectability and proclaimed a theoretically justified position. Each found his own constituency among the people, and each was surrounded by a coterie of devoted followers. As the Revolution increased in violence and chaos, the positions of the leading revolutionaries became more sharply defined. It was as if small beleaguered islands, each with its own ruler, were beginning to form in the turbulent sea of the Revolution. With the threat of war inside and outside France's borders the façade of revolutionary unity cracked and a schism opened up between the more radical 'Men of the Mountain' and the heterogeneous but basically more moderate Girondins. The elimination of the latter was followed by a break-up into increasingly smaller factions, each terrified of undergoing a fate similar to that of the Girondins.

Beneath the upper echelon of leadership was another layer in the power structure consisting of those deputies given licence to prosecute the Revolution throughout the country and dispense revolutionary justice where necessary. Among these representatives-on-mission, as they were called, were some of the Revolution's most depraved characters. These were men who avidly grasped the authority given to them by the National Convention and set about their task with sadistic zeal.

The Terror was introduced as a nationwide policy, but its local application was capriciously determined by the individual proclivities of the representatives-on-mission. While some parts of the country were relatively untouched, others fell into the clutches of men who did not scruple to commit mass murder in the name of revolutionary justice. High up in the hierarchy of notoriety was the deputy Jean-Baptiste Carrier, whose operations in Nantes resulted in the deaths of several thousand prisoners taken during the Civil War in the Vendée. Many of these were executed by the guillotine or shot. Others were bound together and towed out into the river Loire on barges which were then sunk.

Another atrocity was the formation of 'hell columns' *(colonnes infernales)*, groups of captive 'suspects' forced to march across the countryside in parallel columns and then bayoneted to death. 'One will act likewise with women, girls and children', wrote the general in charge of this operation, Turreau. The Committee of Public Safety in Paris, in response to his request for approval for this action, declared his actions 'good and pure, but, far from the theatre of operations, we await results before judging . . . Exterminate the brigands down to the last one. That is your duty.' And there were many similar episodes in which people of the regions caught up in the Civil War were rounded up as suspects and done to death with scant or no regard for evidence of their innocence or guilt. These actions call to mind the mass killings of the twentieth century euphemistically referred to as 'ethnic cleansing'.

The mind sets of those who perpetrated these atrocities are hard to fathom. Carrier appears to have worked himself up into a state of rage while the killings were going on. One observer reported seeing him shouting at his officers to 'kill and kill' and to 'butcher the children without hesitation'. Another deputy, Joseph le Bon, a former priest from Arras, travelled around his region accompanied by his own portable guillotine and was described as becoming feverishly excited during the executions. His particular specialty was to turn the occasion into a triumphal ceremony in which his victims were forced to listen to a speech from him, with the band playing the revolutionary song *Ça Ira* before they were finally dispatched.

Several streams of reasoning and emotionality appear to have flowed together to create these savage acts. These were men who found themselves in positions of unrestrained power and exulted in its intoxicating effects. They had been given permission and relieved of their fear of disapproval by a higher authority in the form of the Committee of Public Safety. By the same token they harboured the fear of being punished by that all-powerful body (which of course meant death) if they disobeyed its injunctions.

Freed of the burden of personal responsibility they could give uninhibited expression to the sadistic urges which fear of disapproval normally kept at bay. Whether they committed their acts in a state of callous detachment, sadistic relish or orgiastic frenzy, they lacked the ability to feel the suffering of their victims. Compassion, empathy and identification with the 'other' were not part of their emotional vocabulary. Instead, their outpourings of rage and hate had been given psychological authority by the political leadership of the moment and moral authority by the belief, again reinforced from on high, that they were being true to the ideals of the Revolution.

How did the groups which serviced the Terror choose their leaders? The effect of emotional surges on groups is to unify them, regardless of the particular emotion. Fear and rage announce danger and prompt people to turn to one another in search of protection. The mood of euphoria, with its concomitant mind-set of hope, also has a unifying effect. People turn to one another in a spirit of celebration at the prospect of being lifted out of a dire predicament.

A group chooses as its leader someone who is perceived as meeting the predominating need of the moment. A group in which the sense of danger prevails will choose a leader capable of identifying the source of that danger and then destroying it, or if that is not possible, leading the group towards safety. When hope is the emotion uppermost in the group's mind a leader is chosen who promises to relieve the group of its suffering and deliver it into a new world. Such leaders conjure up a vision of the future replete with all the ingredients, material and spiritual, which are being denied to them in the bleak world which they happen to inhabit.

The leaders of the Revolution encompassed both these elements in varying proportions. The great pressure on them was to preserve the illusion of unity. At all costs the Revolution had to be presented as a movement which represented the Will of the People, those very people who had been grandly proclaimed as sovereign and indivisible. This meant that the emotions which raged within and among the people had somehow to be rendered compatible with the vision.

There could not be more than one interpretation of the Revolution. But whose interpretation was the correct one? All had to agree, but this could only happen if the discourse was confined to the vision, the Rousseau-esque dream, not its various interpretations. As soon as an attempt was made to get into specifics the debate entered a quagmire.

The reality of course was that each of the revolutionary leaders spoke with a different voice, and each voice resonated with a different constituency. Some, the more embittered and enraged among the leaders, spoke directly to those who had been most traumatized by their sufferings; others, who were more interested in abstractions and ideals, found their audience in a more moderate constituency. Some spoke of bread, others of utopia. All, however, spread the culture of blame and fear if their particular creed was not upheld.

Robespierre led a charmed life for so long because he managed to assemble all these elements in his flowery pleas to the people. His grandiloquence was music to both the wretched of the earth and the theoreticians of the Revolution. In his mind it was entirely possible to reconcile the dream of a virtuous society with the nightmare of the Terror. In his words, 'If the mainspring of popular government in peacetime is virtue, amid revolution it is at the same time both virtue and terror: virtue, without which terror is fatal; terror, without which virtue is impotent. Terror is nothing but prompt, severe, inflexible justice; it is therefore an emanation of virtue.'

In the hierarchy of the emotions, terror and rage form the primitive base of an evolutionary pyramid which unites us through hardwired reflexes with the animal kingdom. Above these are the subtle gradations of affect which impart to us our uniquely human character: Fear shades into anxiety which gives us our ability to experience doubt and inner conflict; while rage cools into anger, a more focused and contained emotion which accompanies an awareness of otherness. The emotion-laden senses of shame and guilt rely on our ability to imagine how others might see us and our capacity for self-reflection.

Higher still on the evolutionary scale is the range of emotions which accompany our ability to feel for others, to hold them in mind, as it were. Respect, empathy, compassion and altruism are all terms by which we acknowledge our ability to identify with others. This ability enables us to value our differences, including the fact that we belong to different groups. The concepts of Liberty, Fraternity and Equality as enshrined in the revolutionary Declaration of the Rights of Man were the first rough-hewn expressions of these emotions. So too was the morality encompassed in Robespierre's Republic of Virtue, a morality created by men entranced by a dream but still lacking the emotional wherewithal to translate their dream into a reality. The Revolution gave birth to an altruistic political doctrine which did not have to be justified by religious belief.

Both the violence and the creativity of the Revolution were driven by group emotions. The collision between an old world encrusted with feudal traditions and a new world infused with the creative thoughts of the Enlightenment resulted in an explosive release of contradictory emotions. Emotions in groups follow the same dynamic principles as they do in individuals. An individual within a given group invests the other individuals and the group itself with emotional charges acting like messengers from the self to the other, which sink, like Cupid's arrows or poisoned darts, into the substance of the other.

Members of the group become connected through a network of communication channels which bind them together and give them their collective identity as a group. One might imagine these liberated emotions seeking out new targets, or 'objects', combining with new thoughts and condensing into new ideas which became contained within new groups.

The carriers of emotion are the acts, gestures and words by means of which we communicate with our fellow human beings. The leaders of the Revolution, many of whom were lawyers and orators well before they ever set foot in the nation's legislature, were past masters at whipping up the emotions which matched their political designs.

When Robespierre spoke of 'terror' he did not mean a state of paralyzing fear but a judicially sanctioned act of intimidation, the instillation of fear as a political device. And virtue was, in Robespierre's book, the ardent upholding of a lifestyle in keeping with the high moral standards of a peaceful democratic society as enunciated in the Declaration of the Rights of Man. The latter, however, was not so easy to legislate for. It was easier to pick up defaulters (and this included those who were not 'ardent' or enthusiastic enough in their espousal of virtue) and subject them to the 'justice' demanded by the Terror. We see in his speeches the creeping use of euphemisms which was to colour the vocabulary of latter-day totalitarian leaders.

It is worth pausing a moment to reflect on the confused emotions of this man who believed until his dying moment that everything he did was within the spirit of the law which he held so dear. In the absence of love (and here we can include all those emotions which sustain the value of the 'other') law is all there is to protect us from the naked abuse of power.

By conflating terror with justice and coupling it with virtue Robespierre managed to wrestle the whole crazy logic of his mind into a coherent policy in which Terror and Virtue stood as the twin pillars of a new revolutionary ideology. The tragedy and irony of the situation is that his cockeyed perspective resonated with the minds of so many of those in power, who avidly embraced it and held it up as the justification to perpetrate the atrocities which still haunt the Revolution.

Rapid organization of thinking and action was needed to ward off the danger which threatened from the liberated emotions. This meant the construction of a system of thought which could preserve the newly emergent group self of the Revolution. The division which had crystallized early on in the Revolution, between 'patriots' (the group 'self') and 'enemies of the people' (the group of the 'other'), became more pronounced as the Revolution ran increasingly out of control. As fear spread, the former group shrank and the latter group enlarged. Fewer comrades could be trusted as patriots, while the ranks of the enemy swelled proportionately.

The group dynamic which prevailed during the Reign of Terror is best understood by the concept of 'paranoia'. This is a term which has had a roller-coaster history through psychiatry, psychoanalysis and popular culture. Essentially, it refers to the mind's simplistic solution to the problem of 'badness', which involves expelling what is perceived as bad from the self and locating it elsewhere (in the 'other'). In psychodynamic terms the bad elements of the self are projected elsewhere but not lost. The bad 'other' becomes a repository for these projections and has to be watched, kept under scrutiny as it were, in case it chooses to return and take revenge for the expulsion.

A paranoid group dynamic is one in which those inside the group battle to protect themselves from those outside who are perceived as enemies. Such groups are endemic in human relationships. They impinge on our lives with a diversity which ranges from family jealousies to petty business rivalries to large-scale social conflict and global warfare. The paranoid dynamic reflects a state of mind in which there is a clear belief that 'good' is located within the group self and 'bad' within the other group. The conflicts which arise across this divide are usually destructive to both the self and the other, based as they are on assumptions which often have little or no bearing on reality.

Paranoia is not only about the exaggerated fear of persecution, it is about a grandiose sense of self-importance. It is accompanied by a wish to put something right, to restore justice, to heal, save or rescue others. In its extreme manifestation it reaches messianic proportions and becomes the driving force for religious and political fundamentalism.

At its core lies a deep sense of injury to the self which cannot be dealt with except by projecting hurt and anger onto a stage peopled by victims and perpetrators. When the grandiose individual attempts to put his programme into action, the inevitable opposition which results provokes the other side of paranoia, the persecutory mind-set. Rage and fear rise to the surface, get expressed in actions which are directed at the perceived enemy and set in motion a vicious cycle of attack and counter-attack.

When idealization fades, demonization comes into the foreground. The language of betrayal replaces the language of unity, and the spirit of fear replaces the spirit of optimism. In revolutionary France the spirit of optimism had been sinking since the king's flight to Varennes in June 1791. The war of words had escalated into sustained attacks directed at the forces gathering on France's borders, who reciprocated with threats of dire consequences if the royal family was harmed. The outbreak of the war in April 1792 created a collective mind-set dominated by fear of annihilation and rage felt towards those perceived to have betrayed the country.

As in July 1789 and August 1792 the people's rage spilt over into violence, chaotic at first, but increasingly orchestrated. Paris had already been re-organized into sections and a revolutionary Commune had taken the place of the Municipal Authority, but after the prison massacres of September 1792 higher levels of leadership from within the National Convention were called for. As each wave battered against the doors of the legislature those within were driven to adopt desperate measures to contain the violence, partly by placating the perpetrators by acceding to their demands, partly by appropriating control and trying to prove themselves capable of managing the people's grievances.

The deputies were split between those who were more in sympathy with the raging masses at the gates and those who saw in them the dark forces of anarchy and destruction. But revolutionary doctrine had determined that there could be no splits between the representatives of the people. They were one and indivisible, splitting was factious, and faction was a crime against the state. However the reality of disagreement would not go away by uttering the mantras of the Revolution. The clash between the rosy dream of unity and the grim reality of diversity was about to be played out the inner sanctum of the legislature, the National Convention.

By June 1793 the Deputies of the National Convention were huddled together inside a shrinking magic circle. War against other nations, civil war and legalized bloodshed were raging around them. The king had been killed but no one had yet dared to lay hands on the sacred representatives of the people. After all, they were the representatives of the sovereign people, and were the people not sacred? But the crowd was pressing at the gates of the sacred temple. There was a growing clamour and a call for action to solve the very real practical problems of imminent starvation. The basic flaw in the revolutionary logic, the insistence on refusing to allow differences of opinion, was beginning to show through the haze of an idyllic unity. Failure to resolve the problems of the day heralded the return of the scapegoat dynamic.

The context for this lay in the vicious quarrels which had broken out at the beginning of 1792 over the conduct of the war against France's enemies. This was personified in the antagonism between Jacques Pierre Brissot, a journalist and orator who dominated the Legislative Assembly, and Robespierre. These men detested each other, and each of them served as a focus of factional leadership.

Brissot, despite his advocacy of a policy of war, belonged to the more 'moderate' faction, moderate in the sense of wanting to achieve some form of political solution which would include the king as a constitutional monarch. Robespierre's view was that a declaration of war would be unwise because victory would mean giving credit to the king and defeat would mean the destruction of the Revolution.

On this occasion Robespierre's view had proved unpopular. The declaration of war and the first shock defeats of the French army which opened up a realistic possibility that Paris could be taken pushed the levels of panic and paranoia to new heights. For four days in September 1792 the streets of Paris were taken over by gangs of murderers going from prison to prison and indiscriminately butchering the inmates, political suspects, non-juring priests and ordinary criminals alike. Most of those killed were dragged through a farcical process of summary trial before tribunals before being taken out and done to death.

The September massacres, as they came to be known, sent shock waves through France and the rest of Europe. The man chiefly responsible for inciting them was a journalist with an unquenchable hatred for aristocrats and counter-revolutionaries, Jean Paul Marat. His journalistic outpourings through his paper 'The People's Friend' and his ranting oratory were filled with invective and calls for the blood of the enemies of the Revolution. Devoid of political shrewdness, he nevertheless sounded a chord with the most desperate and enraged members of the Parisian sections and the Paris Commune, and his moment came when the anger of Paris welled up into another torrent, this time spilling over into the legislative chamber which housed the Legislative Assembly.

Groups which are starkly split between good and evil choose as their enemies those who emerge into the foreground as posing the greatest threat to their survival. Martyrs are appointed by the 'good' group and demonized by the 'bad' group. Scapegoats are often represented as martyrs, even though their stance may have been one of passivity, bewilderment, or frank innocence of the reasons for their choice as scapegoats. But the boundary between the two roles is blurred. Louis XVI was destroyed by the Revolution. In one sense he was the scapegoat, innocent of the crimes of his forebears, in another sense he was taken up as a martyr in the Royalist cause. In yet a third sense he was neither, simply a man responsible through his personal failings and inaction for his fate.

One man's martyr is another man's demon. In the war between Good and Evil, where the alternatives are presented as devoid of middle ground or compromise, the group constructs its heroes as martyrs, its victims as scapegoats. With the collapse of the middle ground and paranoia rampant a banner was hoisted proclaiming that those who believed in compromise and moderation were hypocrites. Soon the cry went out: Anyone who was less than enthusiastic about the Revolution or who fell short of the ideals of good citizenship would be bracketed with the enemy.

The machinery of the Terror began to crank, slowly at first, but with an escalation in the number of cases tried, persons found guilty and death sentences passed. In tandem with the Political Terror came the Religious Terror. This too had its emotional origins in the collision between the old and new worlds which opened the Revolution. In the eyes of the passionate devotees of the Enlightenment the Catholic Church had colluded shamefully with the *ancien regime* in perpetuating tyranny and exploitation. In the early flushes of legislation the

Church had been stripped of much of its wealth. Many of the humbler clergy had sympathy with this, but the revolutionaries were not content with mere material acquisitions. To them the Revolution was an alternative religion which could brook no shared loyalty.

To dismantle so colossal a structure as the Church would take time, and as with the assault on the Monarchy, there was no concerted policy to overthrow it at first. In those critical times policies had to be invented on the hoof. The only guiding light was the increasingly hazy vision of a new society. Nevertheless, divided loyalties were easily rendered into the polarities of revolutionary and counter-revolutionary, and a simple solution would be to bind the clergy to the new state with an oath of loyalty. Inevitably this exaggerated the split in the clergy between those who saw it as their moral duty to join the Revolution and those who would not renounce their primary loyalty to the Church. With the advent of the Reign of Terror these so-called refractory clergy were shuffled off into the enlarging ragbag category of counter-revolutionaries, royalists and foreigners who were given the collective identity of enemies and traitors.

In a paranoid group, the search for new scapegoats buys more time, especially when it is backed by power. The Reign of Terror succeeded as far as it did because those who masterminded it had perfected the art of blaming others for the failings of the Revolution. It failed when it did because the enlarging group of enemies whom it created were not content to become the next batch of passive victims led to the slaughter. Power was draining out of the dominant group. The promises of its leaders that it was simply a matter of time before the last enemies of the Revolution were eliminated and that the republic of virtue was just around the corner acquired a hollow ring.

The fight had been about ownership of the Revolution. Whose interpretation of the Revolution was correct? Revolutionary doctrine had it that there could only be one interpretation – the will of the people, single and indivisible. The individual's right to speak out had been destroyed. In the words of Robespierre and St Just, anyone who spoke out against the will of the people was guilty of treason.

But who were the custodians of the people's will? The answer lay with the small group who held power. And the group was getting smaller, and exercising tighter control on society. The Committee of Public Safety was, in effect, the Inner Circle of the Revolution, the Collective High Priests who were there to interpret the direction and meaning of the Revolution. It was almost a closed order and Robespierre was its High Priest, there to interpret the Revolution to the masses. Enlightenment and education were all that was needed. There were those too stupid and selfish to realize the blessing which had been bestowed on them. If they could not be enlightened they would have to be eliminated; they were traitors to the cause.

The Reign of Terror had cast a long shadow. But there was a message of hope in its brevity. The people were sick of blood. They no longer swallowed the myth of a pervasive enemy. Cries of dismay and shock at the youthfulness and manifest innocence of some of the victims could be heard. The ploy of mixing common criminals with political dissidents and executing them *en masse* no longer worked. 'We do not thirst for blood, we thirst for justice' was the defensive proclamation of Danton. And one of his henchmen, Thuriot, proclaimed, 'We must check this torrent, which is sweeping us back to barbarism'. The shedding of more and more blood hardly seemed the best way to achieve justice.

Against them, St Just, in an anarchic diatribe, opened up yet another split, between the people and the government itself. Authority, he said, should be dispersed until it became identified with the revolutionary movement. The people of a free society ought to be able to regulate their own affairs without the direction of a superior authority. This was a psychotic vision of an ideal democracy and had as its terrible implication the belief that if such freedom could not be immediately established it was the fault of all those who refused to identify with the revolutionary movement. These people had to be eliminated as enemies.

In the face of this all-consuming paranoia, what was to become of the nation, beleaguered now from within itself? The seething crowds had been subdued, harnessed into the military service of the country. The people were cowed and intimidated. The threat of invasion had receded and panic had subsided, but dull disillusionment had taken its place. Apathy, in itself a revolutionary sin, stalked the streets.

The individual had been reduced to a sullen, conformist, paranoid person, morbidly watchful of himself and others, programmed to check his every mannerism and utterance, what he said to whom and in what spirit. With hindsight we can see the spectre of totalitarianism on the horizon. The people had been informed that they should be manifestly deliriously happy, as was expected of good revolutionaries. If they did not adhere to this injunction, they realized that they could be branded as enemies of the people, with fatal consequences.

Despite promises, there had been no magical transformation of France into a land of peace and plenty. Prices of essential foodstuffs continued to climb, enemy troops still threatened destruction, young men were being torn from their labours in the countryside to serve in the national army and the revolutionary government was, it seemed, still tolerating the hoarders, speculators and royalists who had been

128 | THE REIGN OF TERROR

responsible for people's suffering in the first place. The group dynamic of the scapegoat had returned with a vengeance.

In the chronicles of civilization it is possible to discern our never-ending struggle as human beings to gain mastery over the raw emotions which link us to the rest of the animal kingdom. Fear and rage, the emotions needed for our physical survival, also happen to work against the discovery of creative solutions for society's conflicts unless they can be modified by our powers of reasoning and intellect.

Similarly, emotional states such as euphoria, ecstasy and serenity, which confer on us our sense of well being, must be transformed by our reasoning faculties into future-orientated concepts like hope and idealism if they are to serve the interests of the wider society. Given full rein, our emotions bring us closer to our animal-like state. Conversely, judgments made in the absence of felt emotion produce delusional beliefs which are as destructive to society as the actions which spring from unbridled emotion. Immersion in either of these two extreme states of mind renders us incapable of self-reflection and empathy.

CHAPTER NINE

The Power of the Group
to Destroy its Leader
The Fall of Robespierre

'The sovereignty of the people demands that the people be unified;
it is therefore opposed to factions, and all faction is a
criminal attack upon sovereignty.'
St Just, 10th March 1794

Louis XVI, the pious misfit in whose person the sovereignty of France had resided, was dead. With his disappearance from the scene, sovereignty had passed, not to one person, but to the whole nation. But the theory enshrined in Rousseau's vision of an enlightened society was fraught with complexities not anticipated by the leaders of the Revolution. It would take only seven more years for sovereignty to settle once more on the head of one person and for the dream of a new, democratic society to fade into the background.

Between the glorious days of 1789 and the death of Robespierre in 1794 power in France sluiced around between different groups, all claiming sovereign authority in the wake of the new-found coronation of the people. Louis had been impervious to the power of emotion in lifting people's hopes or dashing them to the ground. A wiser monarch would have seen the solemn procession which announced the opening of the States General as the funeral of an old world and welcomed the opportunity to inaugurate a new one with words of inspiration. But Louis had seriously misjudged the significance of the occasion. Within days he had squandered a large store of goodwill, first by humiliating the third estate in the ceremonial proceedings and then by disappointing them with a display of intransigence which augured badly for a co-operative relationship.

The States General expired almost as soon as it had been resuscitated. Its three feudal chambers had collapsed into one. Now, instead of three segregated groups there was a single integrated group, calling itself the National Assembly. A mood of excitement dominated this assembly, as one decree after another unravelled the oppressive laws of the *ancien regime*. Eloquent orators like Mirabeau and Sieyès inspired the deputies with a historic sense of their mission. The power of rhetoric as an instrument of change was beginning to be felt.

The National Assembly quickly became a Constituent Assembly, charged with the task of designing a new constitution. Once this had been achieved, the Constituent Assembly dissolved itself and elections were held for a Legislative Assembly to carry forward the work embodied in the new constitution. Moderation still prevailed, but the new assembly was fatally weakened by a law which prevented anyone who had been a deputy in the previous assembly from standing for election.

This so-called self-denying ordinance, promoted by Robespierre, was intended to prevent the entrenchment of power through prolonged office. Its effect, however, was to deprive the assembly of the hard-fought experience gained by the original deputies. In Robespierre's mind we can imagine an idea flickering that the way to block tyranny was to give as many people as possible the right to represent the people, since power held for too long by too few could only be abusive.

Despite his exclusion from the forum of the new Legislative Assembly by virtue of his own self-denying ordinance, Robespierre did not lose a moment in continuing his fight elsewhere. New power bases had been established in the political clubs which had sprouted in the new climate. Robespierre was in his element at the Jacobin club of Paris, where he and other leading revolutionaries refined their demagogic techniques, rehearsed their ideas and marked out their enemies for future destruction. When the Legislative Assembly had run its course, Robespierre would be ready to continue his struggle once again as an elected deputy of the people.

Beneath all formally constituted groups lie hidden groups, constellations of people united by a theme or purpose which does not fit comfortably into the Procrustean bed of a formal group. Beneath the single group of the unified parliamentary chamber lay two groups which had yet to crystallize into their formal structures.

There were those who were advancing a new theoretical justification for change, and those who were justifying the retention of their privileges by the traditions of blood ties or their ordination by God. It was not long before the group advocating change identified itself as the 'patriots' and referred to the other group as the 'enemies of the people.' France was splitting into two factions, with those designated as enemies of the people falling out of the frame of the new society. Soon they would not exist except as enemies, undeserving of their human rights and even their right to live. There would be little to separate enemies of the people from a category of 'other' yet to be invented. In the paradise envisaged by Robespierre the closest he could come to this was the vague conception of foreignness embodied in the term 'counter-revolutionary'.

Many aristocrats had seen the writing on the wall. A trickle of emigration became a flood, and a nucleus of counter-revolutionary activity formed outside France which would fuel the paranoia of the revolutionaries with visions of attack and betrayal. Meanwhile the king remained trapped in France, unhappily suspended between his nominal leadership of the Revolution and his leadership of a growing force of counter-revolutionaries both inside and outside France calling on him to crush the Revolution. The man and his role were being split apart, while his power was ebbing away.

The power of outside forces now began to work against the Legislative Assembly. The enemies of the Revolution in Austria, Prussia and England threatened war, creating a further split in the revolutionary leadership between those who felt that war would be playing into the hands of Louis XVI and those who wanted to go to war in order to carry the Revolution into other countries. The so-called 'moderates' who dominated the assembly chose to advocate war and concentrated their attacks on the radicals, failing to take into account the powerful support for the radicals in Paris. The main constituencies of moderate support lay in provincial France, giving the radicals ammunition to attack the moderates with charges of 'federalism'. This implied a doctrine of fragmentation and dispersion of power contrary to the unified spirit of the Revolution. It effectively tainted the moderates with the stigma of counter-revolution.

Contamination and purity were the primitive fantasies which lurked in the social unconscious of France during the power struggles of 1792. Louis XVI had become irretrievably contaminated by his ill-fated attempt to escape from France. The revolutionary ministers whom he had appointed suffered the same fate by association. The legislative assembly, too, was contaminated by its association with the king. The world of 'pure' revolutionaries, those true to the ideals of the Revolution, was shrinking. In this paranoid atmosphere Robespierre came into his own. His obsession with hunting down those who had 'corrupted' the Revolution sounded a crystal-clear note of resonance with the tense, embittered people of Paris who feared for their lives at the hands of invading armies and saw a traitor in every foreigner or for that matter anyone who was lukewarm about the Revolution.

When war broke out in the spring of 1792, early French setbacks raised xenophobia to a new pitch. On 10th August the end of the monarchy came with a massive surge by an armed crowd which drove the king and his family from their palace into the building where the assembly was meeting and resulted in the massacre of the Swiss troops guarding him. A republic was declared and the royal family imprisoned. During the first days of September another wave of mass hysteria and paranoia triggered an indiscriminate massacre of prison inmates assumed to be agents of counter-revolution, many innocent people among them.

The Legislative Assembly, which had started on a note of optimism, ended its period of government with the country in a state of war with France's external enemies and on the brink of civil war, having failed to save either the king or the group of moderate deputies who had been identified by their Jacobin enemies as traitors. Robespierre, the Incorruptible, was acclaimed hero of the day.

From the start of the Revolution there was a tension between what we might now call 'people power', effectively a form of direct representation, and official power – indirect or delegated representation. As the Revolution unfolded a gap opened up between these two forms of power, which at the height of the Terror had become a chasm. Robespierre had started out his journey as a vociferous champion of direct representation but soon became bogged down in a dilemma as he discovered the price of conceding unlimited power to disparate groups of people who insisted on trampling over his sacred fences in their demands for democracy.

The roots of his decline and fall lay in his conflict over whether to align himself with the forces of parliamentary democracy or the increasingly disaffected forces of extra-parliamentary democracy clamouring for ever more radical change. Both groups represented the sovereign people, and he represented both groups. He found himself in an impossible situation.

The revolutionaries had been determined that no tyrant would ever rise again from the ashes of the *ancien regime* to assert absolute rule. In the spirit of the sovereignty of the people France would only be led by groups, not by individuals who could later re-invent themselves as dictators.

When necessity demanded the presence of a single figure to achieve order at meetings, as in the case of the National Convention with its more than seven hundred deputies, an incumbent president could only occupy the chair for two weeks before handing it over to his successor. With such a system in place power could be rapidly circulated, and no one could turn the chair into a throne. In future, it was believed, the people of France would be led by groups, not individuals.

To cope with the overwhelming tasks of government, the National Convention appointed two more groups, a Committee of General Security and a Committee of Public Safety, each with its specialized areas of responsibility. Of these, The Committee of Public Safety swiftly rose to dominance and began, Frankenstein-like, to control its master. Power soon became concentrated in this group of twelve zealous deputies, Robespierre among them.

The National Convention took on the aspect of a rubber-stamping machine, listening spellbound to the speeches of leading Committee members as they enunciated their new laws and policies to the assembly of anxious, largely uncommitted deputies. Robespierre was the foremost spokesman for the Committee. He moved tirelessly between the green baize table of the Committee room and the podium of the assembly hall, brimming with plans for rooting out the enemies of the Revolution.

Robespierre was the most powerful man of the Revolution, yet paradoxically he held no formal appointment as a leader. He exercised power but he held no high office. It was true that he had been elected as a deputy to the National Convention, but there he was only one of seven hundred. It was also true that he was a member of the most powerful committee in France, but this still does not explain his rise to dictatorial power. To understand this more fully it is necessary to widen the focus and take into the picture the extra-parliamentary groups in which his power also lay.

Since both the Convention and the Committee for Public Safety were groups without leaders, the fight for leadership was carried on both inside and outside the Convention and its Committee. Robespierre's reputation as someone who understood the needs and fears of the people stood high in the political clubs, the Paris Commune and the Sections of Paris. Quite simply, he had powerful friends outside the Convention, including the most extreme elements of the Revolution.

Although he lacked any formal title of leader, his dedication to the cause of the Revolution, combined with his talents as an orator and his ability to expound revolutionary doctrine, had earned him the position of *de facto* leadership. The Committee of Public Safety relied on him to influence the National Convention, which in turn relied on him to keep the restive masses at bay and to sustain the case for the Revolution through times of danger and travail.

Despite his elevated status Robespierre's power was hemmed in by the fact that the Committee of Public Safety remained subordinate and accountable to the National Convention. At the end of the day his power was based on his personal attributes, and it was these that would determine his success or failure in the face of mounting attacks from his enemies. Whoever could dominate the National Convention, the legally enshrined representative body of the sovereign people, would carry the day. And voices would be the only weapons.

By the summer of 1794 the methods to deal with danger and travail were wearing thin with the revolutionary masses. Arrests, intimidation and large-scale executions had produced a widening circle of victims, their families and friends. There was already a core of hostile counter-revolutionary elements waiting in the wings to recover their lost political and religious rights, not to mention their lost possessions. Legislation to address suffering and hardship had failed abysmally. The so-called Law of the Maximum, which placed a ceiling on wages and prices, had done nothing to alleviate the shortages of essential foods and had only succeeded in antagonizing the producers and workers who were hardest hit.

It was a bad time for anyone to withdraw from the political scene if they wanted their views to prevail, but, strangely, this was what Robespierre did. His behaviour in the six weeks preceding his downfall would serve as an object lesson for politicians on how not to steer a course through a crisis. Inexplicably, he stopped attending meetings of both the Committee of Public Safety and the National Convention. Perhaps the strain of having to deal with the murderous quarrels and abusive exchanges flaring up in these groups which he revered as representing the law was becoming too much for him. It is also likely that the inner conflict created by the inconsistencies of his political position was coming to a head, making him increasingly tense and pushing him to the edge of a breakdown. If there was a tactical purpose to his withdrawal, it was obscure and sadly misconceived. He could not see that his support was draining away and that his absence was giving strength to his enemies. Paranoia reigned supreme, and rumours flourished that he was plotting with his cronies behind closed doors. The fact that he was not *hors de combat* through some form of psychological breakdown is attested to by his continuing attendance at the Jacobin Club, whose membership he could still count on to receive him warmly. But even there his behaviour smacked of self-destruction. He denounced people by name – effectively pronouncing a death sentence on them – and ranted against unnamed traitors, a move which sent his known opponents scurrying to protect themselves and plot against him. He alluded darkly to intriguers within the Convention, and spurned an offer of mediation with his fellow deputies, making it clear that he intended to deal with any opposition, including that from within the Committee of Public Safety, by appealing over its head to the National Convention as the ultimate court of the people. Paranoid thinking and emotional isolation feed off each other and he was becoming increasingly paranoid and isolated.

He returned to the Convention on 26th July (8th Thermidor in the revolutionary calendar), to deliver a well-prepared speech which lasted for two hours. His terminal mental state is painfully transparent in both the content of this speech and the way in which he delivered it. True to form, he began with a long-winded preface in which he re-visited his favourite themes: His glowing vision of a republic of virtue just over the horizon and a plea for one final effort to eradicate the remaining enemies of the Revolution, the scoundrels and monsters who were still blocking the path to the promised land. The idyllic and the catastrophic were presented as stark alternatives, dependent on the triumph or destruction of the hostile forces at work.

The language of the speech was characteristically melodramatic and impassioned, but his voice was strangely detached, betraying a high pitch of tension and a disconnectedness between his ideas and his emotions. He read from his manuscript in a measured, unchanging voice out of keeping with the emotive rhetoric of the content, blinking nervously and drumming his fingers on the rostrum as if impatient with himself. The mannerisms were those of a man suffering acute inner conflict.

He went on to offer himself, with a grandiose flourish, as a martyr to the cause of the Revolution. This was not the first time he had done so, but on this occasion there was a defiant and self-pitying accent on the offer. It was as if he was challenging his enemies to come and get him, inviting them to help him to commit suicide and achieve immortality. In phrases ringing with irony he declared that he was being blamed for everything. He was, he said, being made responsible for the persecution of priests, nobles and patriots, and for the unjust executions perpetrated by the revolutionary tribunal. Nameless people out there were accusing him of being a dictator, he said, adding with sarcastic bitterness that if that was the case, his recent six-week absence from public life must have provided a welcome respite from his alleged dictatorship.

It was as if he knew that this speech was to be his swan song. He had written it as his personal manifesto, a recapitulation of his self-perceived role in the Revolution and his vision of the future. It reads as a dramatic appeal to the people (whoever and wherever they might be at this stage) to save the Revolution.

The speech is a textbook illustration of paranoia – the grandiosity which led him to merge his own being with the Revolution, his perception of a world peopled by enemies who are resorting to disguises, conspiracies and subterfuges in order to pursue their nefarious ends, and his determination to take on his enemies and destroy them or destroy himself in the process. He comforts himself with the thought that 'death is the beginning of immortality' and asks rhetorically: 'If the guilty escape the justice of men, will they escape Eternal Justice, which they have outraged by their horrible excesses?' He is talking about himself and his enemies in the same breath.

The hostile and electrified Convention provided the perfect counterpoint to Robespierre's personal paranoia by displaying its own group dynamic of collective paranoia. His political enemies were feverishly plotting to stop him from denouncing them, while those who did not quite know where they stood in his menacing generalizations were only too ready to throw in their lot with the conspirators. It was the classic self-fulfilling prophecy of the paranoid individual.

Robespierre might have survived longer if he had used his dwindling power to denounce the more dangerous of his enemies sooner, and by name. But he made the fatal mistake of threatening them by insinuation. To compound his mistake he undertook to return to the Convention on the following day with further disclosures. It was a prescription for his own murder, tantamount to an act of suicide. Perhaps he could dimly see that there were more dragons' teeth waiting to sprout after the latest crop of enemies had been eliminated, and had already resigned himself to his own death, or perhaps he still had faith in the Convention to dispense justice on his behalf. After all, was he not the embodiment of the Revolution itself?

He must have been shocked by the icy response at the conclusion of his speech. Instead of the acclamation customarily accorded to his speeches, this one was referred back to the two main executive committees to be re-examined and scrutinized for 'errors', the ominous use of a word which was to creep into the totalitarian language of a later age.

The following morning, in an atmosphere crackling with tension, Robespierre's enemies were waiting for him. It so happened that the president of the assembly for that week was another member of the Committee of Public Safety, Collot d'Herbois, a loud-mouthed, emotionally unstable former actor who had committed spectacular and unbridled atrocities in Lyons. Collot, as he was called, knew that he had incurred Robespierre's displeasure, if only for his rampant attacks on Christian worship. With Collot in charge of the podium it was unlikely that Robespierre would get his opportunity to be heard.

When the crucial debate began, Robespierre's young henchman St Just, began to speak. But the conspirators had anticipated this. He was interrupted on a point of order and accused of speaking only for himself and for Robespierre, not for the committee which he was supposed to represent. Another vociferous enemy of Robespierre, Billaud-Varenne, openly accused Robespierre of plotting against the Convention. His remarks were greeted with applause, and it was clear to the assembly that a fight to the death was in progress.

St Just, normally cool and implacable, froze in the face of these hostile interjections and failed to regain his composure. Robespierre himself now tried to gain the floor, but the conspirators had anticipated this too, and he was attacked with orchestrated shouts of 'Down with the tyrant!' Other speakers were called to the podium instead, each attacking Robespierre in their own way. The final thrust came from another member of the Committee of Public Safety, Bertrand Barère. An eloquent and urbane lawyer, Barère had a reputation for duplicity, and it was said by cynics that he had come to the debate armed with two prepared speeches in his pocket, one to be delivered if the tide seemed to be flowing with Robespierre, the other if it seemed to be flowing the other way. There was no doubt at this point which speech had to be produced.

Through all the shouting and chaos Robespierre tried in vain to gain a hearing. Eye-witness accounts tell that he lost his voice at one point, (or was it perhaps that he could not make himself heard above the din?) provoking the vicious jibe that he was being choked by Danton's blood. One of the ironies of the moment was Barère's accusation that Robespierre had been too vigorous in his defence of Danton.

As the melee continued, the machinery of the Convention's power to arrest one of their own number began to turn. One of the de-Christianizers, an old enemy of Robespierre's, Vadier by name, denounced him for 'indulgence' towards two former victims of the Terror, one of them his childhood friend Desmoulins. Another deputy proposed his arrest and he was hauled before the bar of the tribune to be formally charged.

After having to endure a sanctimonious harangue from the repulsive Collot d'Herbois he was led away, together with four other deputies. His younger brother Augustin and his friend Lebas both stepped forward to be arrested with him. St Just and Couthon, the two members of the Committee of Public Safety identified most closely with him in the popular mind as a dangerous triumvirate, were also arrested, and the five men were dispatched to separate prisons.

But the outcome was still by no means clear. Inside the assembly hall the National Convention had regained its faltering authority and arrested Robespierre, now suddenly re-defined as the man posing the greatest danger to the Revolution. Outside, there were still powerful elements who saw Robespierre as the guardian of the Revolution. These forces were concentrated in the Sections, the districts of Paris controlled by the Commune, the municipal authority of Paris. With the Committee of Public Safety disabled, a showdown loomed between the Convention and the Commune.

The Commune controlled the prisons to which the arrested men were sent, and the jailers, acting on orders, refused to admit them. One by one they were released and made their way to the Hotel de Ville, the headquarters of the Commune, where they ineffectually set about trying to muster support for an insurrection. Yet again Robespierre vacillated fatally. His lawyer's mind could not grasp the fact that he was now on the wrong side of the law, and he had to be urged by his fellows to put pen to paper in an appeal to the citizens of those Paris sections which were loyal to him to seize the moment for an insurrection.

But it was too late. The events of the past year had been more than most Parisians could stomach. They had been battered into a state of sullen apathy by the capricious and escalating implementation of the Terror, and by the hardships imposed on them by the law of the Maximum. The political climate had turned against Robespierre. The usual rallying cry for an Insurrection now fell on deaf ears and none of the five deputies now drifting in limbo commanded enough support to arouse armed action on their behalf. Robespierre and his followers had fallen victim to laws of their own making. On learning of their release the Convention branded them as escapees and declared them 'outside the law', a legal device of St Just which rendered them liable to be put to death after capture and identification, without the formality of a trial.

A few troops loyal to Robespierre did gather outside the city hall, but there were no leaders to give them direction and they lacked the spirit to take any sort of initiative. According to some accounts a heavy downpour of rain was the last straw, and they dispersed into the night, leaving the field clear for the Convention's own hastily mobilized troops. The city hall was broken into and the five fugitives seized. Robespierre suffered a bullet wound to the jaw, and it is typical of the man and the mystery which surrounds him that no one is clear whether this was a self-inflicted wound in a failed suicide attempt, or whether the injury was caused by a shot fired by one of the soldiers entering the room.

Robespierre was carried to the Tuileries and laid down on a table in the anteroom of the Committee of Public Safety. A surgeon tended his wound while spectators pressed around the entrance to gape and taunt. The next morning he was taken in a state of shock to be 'identified' and then put into a tumbril with his brother. The route to the guillotine was lined with jeering crowds. Cries of 'Down with the tyrant!', 'Down with the Maximum!' and obscene vituperations were the sounds that would have reached his ears, if not his dimmed consciousness. His own inarticulate cry of pain was the last sound from him to reach the crowd, as the executioner roughly removed the bandage around his jaw to give the blade of the guillotine surer access.

Until Thermidor the French Revolution had been carried along by two separate and incompatible currents flowing more or less in the same direction. The first stemmed from the spirit of the Enlightenment, with its high-minded ideas embodied in the declaration of human rights. The second, inherited from a more primitive strand of thought, embodied in ideas generated by the fear of destruction and the rage of frustrated basic needs. Now these currents were flowing across each other, creating a cross-current into which Robespierre was sucked. The conflict between these two strands of thought, the enlightened and the barbaric, the noble and the savage, was the great paradox of the Revolution, and also the great paradox of Robespierre, whose mind encompassed both of these contradictory aspects, and whose oratorical skill and intellectual acrobatics enabled him to become the mouthpiece for both. His downfall represents his failure to reconcile them, both to himself and to others.

There is no clear answer to the question of where responsibility lies for the Reign of Terror. Robespierre, with his legal mind, political dedication and paranoid personality was undoubtedly its chief architect. But he did not instigate it single-handedly. He brought his twisted ideas to the elected representatives of the people, who dignified them with legal approbation and gave him the machinery to put them into practice. As soon as he was dead, the politicians who had shared his philosophy rushed to exculpate themselves. They, and the moderate revolutionaries who re-emerged from the shadows, saw in him the perfect scapegoat. The counter-revolutionaries and the many who had lost relatives and friends in the Terror also had no hesitation in reviling him and presenting him to posterity as a monster.

Perhaps Robespierre's undoing lay not in his ruthlessness but in the fact that he was not ruthless enough. He was not a soldier like Napoleon, who blasted his enemies with cannon, but a lawyer, who blasted his enemies with words which he hammered into laws. But despite his introduction of laws which resulted in the deaths of thousands, he was no sadistic killer with a taste for blood. There was no relish, or even satisfaction, at the deaths of those whom he had converted into enemies. If anything, the evidence is that he suffered inwardly and agonized over the decisions which resulted in people's deaths.

CHAPTER TEN

How History and Myth Intertwine

'We must consider how very little history there is:
I mean real authentick history.'
Samuel Johnson

'J'ai vécu.' (I survived)
Sieyès (when asked what he had done during the Revolution)

The conflict which underlay the French Revolution was as much a conflict of opposing mythologies as of political doctrines. On one side was the myth of power and privilege given by God to one ruler and passed down through ties of blood. Ranged against that was the myth of the tyrant who had enslaved the people and the heroes who would liberate them and lead them into a new world in which they would govern themselves and lead virtuous lives.

The drama and tragedy of the Revolution lay in the irreconcilable nature of these myths. One group invoked religion and tradition to support its mythology; the other invoked reason and the innate goodness of the people. The two groups for whom these myths formed the fabric of their collective identity could not co-exist. Neither group could identify with the other and each group saw in the other an alien and dangerous adversary.

Having swept away the rotten structures of feudalism and absolutism, the French Revolution announced the arrival of two new political philosophies – parliamentary democracy and state dictatorship. Both of these doctrines were strains of ideological thought deriving from cells which had been grown in the pure culture of Rousseau's enlightened ideas. Unfortunately these cells could not germinate in the laboratory-like tranquility which they needed. Theory and human nature clashed brutally, and the explosion in France triggered a chain of other explosions across Europe, generating shock waves which battered the continent for the next two hundred years.

Those who were attempting to shape the political destiny of Europe therefore had to contend with, and were influenced by, an uninterrupted torrent of violence in the form of wars, civil wars and further revolutions, all of which produced a fresh crop of victims, survivors and perpetrators of trauma struggling to recover strength and gain power. Everyone was learning lessons from the past, but few lessons found their way into the same textbook.

All who were caught up in the struggles which dominated the Revolution were tainted by their efforts to proclaim themselves as the only purveyors of the truth and all others as false prophets. Faith in the leaders of the Revolution collapsed, and with it, faith in the principles of the Revolution. The search for heroes having proved fruitless despite a hastily constructed martyrology, the Revolution went down in history as a political contradiction, an event in which great groups rose and fell without correspondingly great figures in charge. Those who led these groups had short-lived careers.

The first enduring hero to emerge after the Revolution was Napoleon, who could claim revolutionary credentials but who renounced the revolutionary principle of group leadership after he had restored France to her imagined glory. From that point on leadership resided in military autocracy, as the revolutionary turned soldier turned statesman healed the wounds of his afflicted nation by inflicting them on the rest of Europe.

After the fall of Napoleon the pendulum continued to swing between revolution and counter-revolution. Another empire came and went and a republic arrived for the third time in 1871. Imperial glory translated into nationalistic fervor as the country found itself face to face with another powerful enemy in the form of Prussia and Germany. Violence continued to oscillate between a militaristic Right, promising to rescue the country from chaos and restore order even at the price of personal liberty and a socialistic Left vowing to safeguard the old revolutionary rights even in the teeth of an outside enemy. France was once again locked between two conflicting myths, that of the soldier-saviour who would restore power and glory to a traumatized people and that of an inspired collective voice which would heal the trauma by proclaiming the old virtues of liberty, equality and fraternity.

In 1978 the French historian Francois Furet announced: 'The French Revolution is over.' From then on it was to be treated as history rather than politics. And in 1989 the British historian Norman Hampson supported Furet's position, declaring that the Revolution's bicentenary was 'as good an occasion as any to celebrate its demise as theology and its reincarnation as history'.

But today the French Revolution is still a hot potato. It surfaces, not only in the slogans and imagery of peoples across the world but as a point of reference for political conflict in cases of mass uprising and whenever questions of terror, warfare and assaults on regimes occur. In 2012, in a book titled *In Defence of the Terror*, Sophie Wahnich explains how the instigators of the Reign of Terror sought to contain legitimate popular violence and how this goal was subsequently subsumed in the logic of war. The Terror, she maintains, 'was a process welded to a regime of popular sovereignty, the only alternatives being to defeat tyranny or die for liberty'.

Wahnich is endorsed by the philosopher Slavoj Žižek, who, in his foreword to her book, urges the reader not to reject violence simplistically, but to see it where tyrannical rulers have encrypted it and then to flush it out in the service of freedom. To Žižek and Wahnich the choice is stark: freedom, (the price for which is severe discipline), or death (in conditions of servitude and with loss of dignity).

The argument in favour of the liberating impact of violence stems from a myth that the world is a place where the forces of good and evil are forever in opposition. It provides the justification for war, terror, revolution and political murder. The task which holders of this particular myth give themselves is to identify and destroy the people who represent the embodiment of evil. There is no end in sight and no hope for change through harmonious integration of opposites.

An opposing myth is constructed around the belief that good and evil are not polar opposites lodged inescapably within specific groups of people, but fluctuating entities which wax and wane with the vicissitudes of the contexts in which we live. This myth holds that evil can be kept at bay by the combined efforts of our intelligent capacity for repairing damage and healing hurt.

We all need myths, but because they encroach on our irrational mind they need to be understood and unpicked and their irrationality exposed for what it is.

Let us take an example from the politics of 1931:

WINSTON CHURCHILL: 'We have all heard of how Dr Guillotin was executed by the instrument that he invented.'

SIR HERBERT SAMUEL: 'He was not!'

WINSTON CHURCHILL: 'Well, he ought to have been.'

Churchill's throwaway line on the fate of Dr Guillotin shows how easily myths can be perpetuated by statesmen, in this case an Englishman with an aversion to revolution. In fact the man with the unfortunate surname died peacefully in his bed, hating the opprobrium which clung to him simply because he had refined a medieval executing machine into a rapidly operated device for ending life humanely.

If heads could be sliced off in one fell swoop of an impersonal blade then surely this was a preferable death to the often botched hacking by a clumsy brute wielding an axe or sword. Moreover Dr Guillotin was a democrat who believed that there should be no discrimination between aristocrats and the common people, even on the scaffold. If anything, he deserves credit rather than vilification. But myths have a tenacity which tightens their grip with time.

The further back in time we go the more malleable are the events and personages of the day and the easier it is to turn them into figments of our own imagination. So much has happened between 1789 and 2014 that the eighteenth century feels quaintly disconnected from the modern world. Its history has become telescoped into a series of iconic images and cartoony characters: A king and queen besieged and then executed by bloodthirsty revolutionaries. Who are the goodies and who the baddies? It is quite difficult to tell them apart. They are all so ridiculous.

In this *reductio ad absurdum* of the French Revolution the wider context has been airbrushed out of the picture and all we are left with is a myth suitable for inclusion in a children's book of horrible histories. If we take away the costumes and period props, however, we uncover a story which fits a dozen different social upheavals in today's world. We have to strip ancient myths of their cultural trappings in order to recognize their modern day counterparts.

A popular narrative of the French Revolution is that it is the story of an exploited and oppressed people becoming violent, gaining power, taking revenge, becoming blinded to their own cruelty and greed, crushing their former persecutors and appointing themselves as a superior group with a mission to conquer and achieve wealth and glory. George Orwell wrote about this in *Animal Farm*, with a different revolution in mind.

Another version has the French Revolution as an eruption of animal violence against a God-given world of peace and order in which all creatures occupy their rightful place. This version describes counter-revolution as a battle to restore this world by harnessing the forces of violence to a military machine capable of being controlled by the victors and being used by them in order to extend their sphere of power and influence. Both myths manufacture a happy ending in wealth and glory.

Sadly, however, violence, regardless of its origins in revolution or war, results in trauma. The emotional concomitants of this produce a vicious cycle of revenge and hatred. Ancient myths are constantly being updated to feed these emotions. Hope, comfort and inspiration are given to the victims of recent traumas by dressing these myths in modern clothing.

All myths are reinforced by celebrations and customs which keep them alive. They provide a thread of continuity, a kind of cultural DNA which transmits information in a relatively unchanging form, matching it against new experiences to create a fresh synthesis of present and past designed to serve the needs of the group. They are shaped, not only by great upheavals in nature – famines, floods and epidemics – but by social conflict and violence. Violence and trauma are two sides of the same coin. Conflict arises when certain myths are proclaimed as right and indispensable to the happiness of the group while other myths are pronounced wrong, evil, dangerous or wicked and deserving of obliteration from human consciousness.

Since myths come attached to real people it is a short step from denouncing a myth to urging the destruction of the people who cherish it. Santayana and Freud warned that those who choose to forget the past are doomed to repeat it, but it is the monolithic interpretation of the past, not just the forgetting of it, which leads to its re-enactment.

Traumatic events which go back centuries are kept alive in the collective mind, transmuted by time into myths whose function is to remind, inform and protect the group. Every culture has its array of heroes, villains and epic struggles woven into a single tapestry in which the threads of myth and history blend to give the group its identity and its link it with the past.

The emotional impact of trauma on people's lives only began to dawn on the civilized world when the horrors of two twentieth-century world wars came to light. Before that, the term 'trauma' (the word literally means 'piercing') referred specifically to tissue injury, and was confined to the provinces of medicine and surgery. The First World War, with its processions of zombie-like casualties repeatedly and wordlessly re-enacting their terrifying battlefield experiences, left psychiatrists groping for a better terminology than 'shell shock' or 'lack of moral fibre' to explain the condition.

When the survivors of the Nazi concentration camps and other atrocities of the Second World War began to tell their stories it gradually became clear that an epidemic of trauma on an unimaginable scale had swept the world and left behind a host of psychological casualties.

A new identity came into being, that of the Survivor, carrying with it a cluster of symptoms which gave it the status of a syndrome. Central to the concept of the Survivor Syndrome was the inability to let go of the past. Memories and images of traumatic experiences forced themselves unbidden into consciousness in the form of flashbacks, intrusive thoughts and nameless fears. Coupled with this was a raw sensitivity to stimuli bearing even a marginal resemblance to the traumatic moment. The sound of a dog barking, for example, might summon up a deeply lodged emotional reaction to the memory of a concentration camp guard dog.

Survivors also suffered from profound existential anxieties about their future and the meaning of the events through which they had lived. Colouring these symptoms was a significantly greater occurrence of the more common emotional symptoms – depression, anxiety and somatic disturbances – and a greater tendency to succumb to severe forms of mental health dysfunction – paranoid thinking, psychotic breakdown and suicide.

Traumatic events are inevitably located within an interpersonal context. Victims of human-induced trauma are haunted by memories of their perpetrators and this leads to a quest for justice and a passion for revenge. Less typically there is a wish to forgive and become reconciled. Underlying these different attempts to alleviate the pain of the trauma is a grim determination to ensure that there will be no repetition of the trauma. Attempts are made to shed the victim role and steps are taken to strengthen those weaknesses seen as having been responsible for the failure to ward off the perpetrator. Former victims seek the power needed to protect them from future would-be perpetrators and fortify the means of attacking and destroying them if necessary.

A common escape route from the victim mentality is sought in the creation of a new identity based on a renunciation of the past and a desire to disown traits perceived as fatally weak. Without realizing it, the former victim is at risk of acquiring the characteristics of the perpetrator, and the stage is set for a cycle of repetition, the recurrence of a drama with the same plot but a different cast. History is fashioned out of these plots.

Works of fiction play their part in the formation of myths. Two examples of this in the perception of the French Revolution by the English-speaking world are: *A Tale of Two Cities* by Charles Dickens and *The Scarlet Pimpernel* by Baroness Orczy.

Dickens, with his wonderful ability to paint word-pictures of grotesque characters and blood-curdling spectacles, has left us with an indelible picture of the French Revolution as an orgy of hatred and bloodshed. Characters like Madame Defarge and the crones who sit with her at the foot of the guillotine, knitting while they gloat over the beheadings, are etched more sharply into our social memory than a dozen real life revolutionaries.

Dickens was not interested in the politics of the Revolution. He was simply revolted by the violence and brutality of it all. We are as much horrified by the spectacle of poor old Dr Manette, tottering out of the Bastille after having been cruelly held prisoner there under the *ancien regime*, as we are by the murderous acts of the peasant *jacquerie,* and we all breathe a sigh of relief when the noble-spirited Charles Darnay is rescued by the sacrificial act of his wastrel look-alike who offers to take his place on the scaffold so that Darnay can be reunited with the woman who loves him. It is the classic Dickensian happy ending, leaving us with the cheerful feeling that the good and the bad have been neatly sorted and that we know what the French Revolution was really all about.

The Scarlet Pimpernel is another book which capitalizes on historical realities. Its popularity lies in its appeal as a swashbuckling adventure story laced with romance, a 'ripping yarn' in which the mysterious hero flits between England and France, playing a dangerous game of diplomacy and intrigue while rescuing victims of the Terror from the guillotine. Because of the visual power of their narratives, both *The Scarlet Pimpernel* and *A Tale of Two Cities* have translated well onto the screen, bringing both stories and their cultural assumptions to a vastly wider audience than the readers of the books.

This brings us to the heart of the conflict about the French Revolution, the discrepancy between spectacle and narrative. The reader might have been matching the stereotyped versions mentioned above with his or her own historical memory of the Revolution. The details would be different, but the chances are that the same two contradictory notions will have surfaced: One based on a recall of high-minded abstractions remembered from history books such as liberty and democracy, the other on emotionally charged images featuring grisly scenes remembered from pictorial illustrations, perhaps from the same books.

Abstractions are difficult to sustain without reference to characters of flesh and blood. Attributions of 'good' and 'bad' settle not only on ideas but on the personalities associated with them. Together they weave the memories and myths which enrich and complicate the historical narrative of the Revolution. The ghosts of many leaders of the Revolution, most of them headless, lurk in the shadows. Historical reductionism has kept them there, and only a very few, perhaps three or four, loom large in today's mythology of the Revolution.

Whatever good they might have done, whatever redeeming nuances sympathetic historians and biographers have been able to tease out of their lives, the central characters of the Revolution remain solidly cast in the popular British mind as demons. Their names are linked with the murders and massacres which accompanied the Reign of Terror and it is almost impossible for us to free ourselves from this association when evaluating their contribution to the Revolution as a force for the greater good. As Lady Macbeth discovered, it is hard to get rid of the smell of blood.

Perhaps this is as it should be. The point of looking more closely at the leaders, the terrible trio of Robespierre, Danton and Marat in particular, is not to rehabilitate them or whitewash their deeds. This would be as much of a travesty of the truth as the relentless and unquestioning typecasting of them as paragons of evil. The point is to try and understand why some societies, in choosing to simplify history and stereotype its characters, have come down so strongly in these cases with a verdict of guilty without any mitigating circumstances while other societies go to the opposite extreme and venerate them as forerunners of a brave new world.

Even before the execution of the king and the Reign of Terror Edmund Burke's *Reflections on the French Revolution* sounded a thunderous note of disapproval at what was going on in France. Leaping to the defence of the Revolution was Thomas Paine, a British-born veteran of the American Revolution whose treatise, *The Rights of Man* (1791) influenced public opinion in England and America.

During the Terror and the Napoleonic wars literary debate on the Revolution disappeared, although survivors, both royalist and revolutionary, were busy with their memoirs which predictably followed the political line with which they had identified themselves during the Revolution. History was a battle of ideas between spokesmen for the rival revolutionary leaders, The nineteenth century saw a battle between apologists for Robespierre and his detractors. To the historian and constitutional monarchist Thiers, for instance, Robespierre was 'one of the most hateful beings who ruled over men'.

Going into the twentieth century, the historian Albert Mathiez regarded Robespierre as a man of unwavering principle, while to Alphonse Aulard, a fellow historian and an ardent Dantonist, he was 'a cold-blooded murderer'. Mathiez's spiritual successors Georges Lefevbre and Albert Souboul, both dedicated leftists, idealized Robespierre as an early socialist, a man who perfected the true revolutionary ideology.

Today's political conflicts between Left and Right are a latter-day resonance of these early conflicts, conflicts between revolutionaries and counter-revolutionaries, between republicans and monarchists, and between those who want to accelerate the pace of change and those who want to retard it.

Ultimately the conflict is between those who embrace the mythology of salvation through the group (the people, the democratic state) and those who embrace the opposite mythology of salvation vested in a single powerful figure (the monarch, the dictator). For the former, destruction comes at the hands of the tyrant, for the latter, destruction comes at the hands of the uncontrolled masses. All who engage with the Revolution are caught between these polarized mythologies and those who study the revolutionary leaders find themselves torn between thinking of them either as representatives of the people and heroes or as tyrants, would-be dictators and monsters.

By the same token some characters are singled out and held in the foreground of collective consciousness, while others recede into the background or disappear entirely, consigned, as Trotsky would have the Mensheviks, to 'the dustbin of history'. This process inevitably involves a degree of distortion and simplification. Myth-making is both conscious, designed to suit the intellectual and political purposes of the makers and unconscious, a product of the emotional life of the group.

The fundamental flaw in the human species lies in its potential to turn on itself, to identify 'Self' as 'Other' and therefore dangerous. This sets in motion a cyclical process of hostility, violence, attack and counter-attack. In a typical sequence of events a group experiences trauma on a large scale (war, disease, famine). The primitive group brain (the network for the social unconscious) detects and registers the trauma by means of imagery, primitive emotions and pre-linguistic thoughts and sends messages to the higher group brain (collective consciousness) alerting it to the danger in the crude language and imagery of fight or flight. The collective consciousness of the group then draws on its extensive archives and predictive capacity, identifies (rightly or wrongly) the source of the trauma and calculates the course of action most likely to save the group.

Having located the threat, the group launches a containing operation, of which the principal technique is segregation. Metaphors of dirt, contamination, defilement, contagion and corruption are set against images of cleanliness and purity. The offending group is separated out from the offended group and then isolated by word and deed, setting the stage for possible expulsion, exploitation or extermination. The path of history is littered with examples of pre-emptive invasion, subjugation, massacre, deportation, forced relocation, detention in camps, and attempts to turn 'Other' into 'Self' by forced conversion. By all these means trauma is inflicted and the cycle of violence is perpetuated.

This depressing view of human group behaviour is tempered by the prospect of discovering ways of interrupting the cycle of violence and reducing the impact of traumatic events. A lobby is needed within society, composed of its less traumatized elements, people who are free enough from the compulsive urges of the primitive brain to work against the principle of attack, vengeance and retaliation as an answer to trauma and in favour of mutual identification and a sense of shared predicament.

The barriers between Self and Other have to be broken down. This does not imply that humanity is a monolithic entity. That way lies totalitarianism. Humanity is diverse and pluralistic by nature. But we have to accept differences and work towards a society as free as possible of human inflicted trauma and concentrate our energies on understanding and mastering the forces of nature which inflict trauma on us.

The French Revolution seems a long way away from the world which saw the rise and fall of Hitler, and even further away from today's world of international power politics, global economics and a form of terrorism which strikes at the soft underbelly of society. But if we accept that modern society is like an organism, we should study its embryology as well as its anatomy and physiology. The French Revolution was an important milestone in our social and political development. We know that it carried within itself the seeds of a humane society, but that it was also a bloody business involving murder and execution on a large scale, and as such a deeply flawed phenomenon. The confusion arising from this Jekyll-and-Hyde dichotomy has echoed down the generations, dividing today's historians, politicians and social commentators with as much passion as it did at the time of the Revolution.

The same split in our thinking applies to our views on all of today's social upheavals and conflicts. Whenever we think about any case of war, revolution or civil strife, we are immediately pulled in two opposite directions. Our 'advanced' brain cross-references with our primitive brain, the part of the brain where pictorial residues from the past are stored and where dreams and images are made and unmade. The new information is matched with pictorial residues from the past and a course of action is determined.

There can be no truly dispassionate account of the Revolution. It was an event which fiercely divided Europe. It shattered a pre-existing world order and gave rise to a new conception of society. Its schisms continue to reverberate through today's scholarly and political discourses, infused with mythical images and beliefs selected to corroborate one or other point of view. Every historian, biographer, artist, social scientist and politician who engages with the Revolution is obliged to dip into its mythology in order to add credibility to a particular point of view. If anything can be learnt from the controversies which still surround the Revolution it is that history and mythology are closely intertwined and that no single version of history and no single myth can claim a monopoly on the truth.

Books which I hope will interest the reader

Best, G. (ed.). *The Permanent Revolution: The French Revolution and its Legacy 1789–1989*. Collins (1988).

Brinton, C. *A Decade of Revolution: 1789–1799*. Harper (1934).

Cobb, R. *The French and their Revolution: Selected Writings edited and introduced by David Gilmour*. John Murray (1998).

Davies, P. *The French Revolution: A Beginner's Guide*. Oneworld (2009).

Doyle, W. *The Oxford History of the French Revolution*. Oxford University Press (1990).

Furet, F. *The French Revolution 1770–1814*. Translated by Antonia Nevill. Blackwell (1996).

Goodwin, A. *The French Revolution*. Hutchinson (1970).

Hampson, N. *A Social History of the French Revolution*. Routledge (1995).

Hampson, N. *Prelude to Terror*. Blackwell (1988).

Haycraft, J. *In Search of the French Revolution: Journeys Through France*. Secker and Warburg (1989).

Hibbert, C. *The French Revolution*. Penguin (1982).

Hobsbawm, E.J. *Echoes of the Marseillaise: Two Centuries Look Back on the French Revolution*. Verso (1990).

Hunt, J. *The French Revolution: Questions and Analysis in History* (eds S.J. Lee and S. Lang). Routledge (1998).

Kennedy, E. *A Cultural History of the French Revolution*. Yale (1989).

Lefebvre, G. *The Great Fear of 1789: Rural Panic in Revolutionary France*. Translated from the French by Joan White. NLB (1973).

McGarr, P. and Callinicos, A. *Marxism and the Great French Revolution*. International Socialism (1993).

Pernoud, G. and Flaissier, S. Preface by André Maurois. Translated by Richard Graves. *The French Revolution*. Secker and Warburg (1960) .

Rudé, G. *The French Revolution*. Weidenfeld and Nicolson (1988).

Schama, S. *Citizens: A Chronicle of the French Revolution*. Penguin (1989).

Steel, M. *Vive La Revolution: A Stand-up History of the French Revolution*. Scribner (2004).

Sydenham, M.J. *The French Revolution*. B.T. Batsford (1969).

Talmon, J.L. *The Origins of Totalitarian Democracy*. Sphere (1951).

Yalom, M. *Blood Sisters: The French Revolution in Women's Memory.* Pandora (1995).

ON LOUIS XVI and MARIE ANTOINETTE
Fraser, A. *Marie Antoinette: The Journey.* Phoenix (2002).
Hardman, J. *Louis XVI.* Yale (1994).
Tackett, T. *When the King Took Flight.* Harvard (2003).
Zweig, S. *Marie Antoinette: The Portrait of an Average Woman.* Translated by Eden and Cedar Paul. Cassell (1935).

ON ROBESPIERRE
Bienvenu, R.T. (ed.). *The Ninth of Thermidor: The Fall of Robespierre.* Oxford University Press (1968).
Carr, J.L. *Robespierre: The Force of Circumstance.* Constable (1972).
Jordan, D.P. *The Revolutionary Career of Maximilien Robespierre.* (University of Chicago 1985).
Hampson, N. *The Life and Opinions of Maximilien Robespierre.* Duckworth (1974).
Hardman, J. *Robespierre: Profiles in Power* (Series) Pearson (1999).
McPhee, P. *Robespierre: A Revolutionary Life.* Yale (2012).
Rudé, G. *Robespierre: Portrait of a Revolutionary Democrat.* Collins (1975).
Scurr, R. *Fatal Purity: Robespierre and the French Revolution.* Chatto and Windus (2006).
Thompson, J.M. *Robespierre and the French Revolution.* English Universities Press (1959).

ON DANTON
Christophe, R. *Danton: a biography* (translated from the French by Peter Green). Arthur Barker and Doubleday (1967).
Hampson, N. *Danton.* Duckworth (1978).
Lawday, D. *Danton.* Jonathan Cape (2009).

ON THE TERROR
Andress, D. *The Terror: Civil War in the French Revolution.* Little, Brown (2005).
Loomis, S. *Paris in the Terror: June 1793–July 1794.* Jonathan Cape (1964).
Mayer, A.J, *The Furies: Violence and Terror in the French and Russian Revolutions.* Princeton (2000).
Palmer, R.R. *Twelve who Ruled: The Year of the Terror in the French Revolution.* Princeton (1970).
Wahnich, S. *In Defence of the Terror: Liberty or Death in the French Revolution.* Verso (2012).

ON CROWDS
Barrows, S. *Distorting Mirrors: Visions of the Crowd in Late Nineteenth-Century France.* Yale (1981).

Canetti, E. *Crowds and Power.* Penguin (1973).

McClelland, J.S. *The Crowd and the Mob: from Plato to Canetti.* Unwin Hyman (1989).

Moscovici, S. *The Age of the Crowd: A Historical Treatise on Mass Psychology.* Translated by J.C. Whitehouse. Cambridge (1985).

Nye, R.A. *The Origins of Crowd Psychology: Gustav LeBon and the Crisis of Mass Democracy in the Third Republic.* Sage (1975).

Rudé, G. *The Crowd in the French Revolution.* Oxford University Press (1959).

Schneider, S. and Weinberg, H. (eds.) *The Large Group Re-Visited: The Herd, Primal Horde, Crowds and Masses.* Jessica Kingsley (2003).

van Ginneken, J. *Crowds, Psychology and Politics, 1871–1899.* Cambridge (1992).

ON THE ENLIGHTENMENT

Himmelfarb, G. *The Roads to Modernity: The British, French and American Enlightenments.* Borzoi (2004).

Hampson, N. *The Enlightenment: An Evaluation of Its Assumptions, Attitudes and Values.* Pelican (1968).

Porter, R. *Enlightenment: Britain and the Creation of the Modern World.* Allen Lane (2000).

Rousseau, Jean-Jacques *The Social Contract.* Translated and Introduced by Maurice Cranston. Penguin (1968).

ON RELIGIOUS BELIEF

Armstrong, K. *The Battle for God: Fundamentalism in Judaism, Christianity and Islam* HarperCollins (2000).

Bergmann, M.S. *In the Shadow of Moloch: The Sacrifice of Children and Its Impact on Western Religions.* Columbia (1992).

Haley, J. *The Power Tactics of Jesus Christ and other essays.* Avon (1969).

James, W. *The Varieties of Religious Experience: A Study in Human Nature.* Fontana (1960).

Sargant, W. *Battle for the Mind: A Physiology of Conversion and Brainwashing.* Malor (1997).

ON TRAUMA

Healy, D. *Images of Trauma: From Hysteria to Post-Traumatic Stress Disorder.* Faber and Faber (1993).

Herman, J. *Trauma and Recovery: The Aftermath of Violence – From Domestic Abuse to Political Terror.* Basic Books (1997).

Volkan, V.D. *Bloodlines: From Ethnic Pride to Ethnic Terrorism.* Farrar, Straus and Giroux (1997).

Volkan, V. D. 'Transgenerational Transmissions and Chosen Traumas: An Aspect of Large Group Identity. *In:* Group Analysis' in *The Journal of Group Analytic Psychotherapy*, Vol. 34, No. 1, March 2001.

ON BIOLOGY AND HUMAN NATURE
Bateson, G. *Steps to an Ecology of Mind.* Paladin (1973).
Goldstein, K. *The Organism. A holistic approach to biology derived from pathological data in man.* NY American Book Company (1939).
Koestler, A. *The Ghost in the Machine.* Hutchinson (1967).
Rose, S. *The Making of Memory: From Molecules to Mind.* Bantam (1993).
Thomas, L. *The Lives of a Cell: Notes of a Biology Watcher.* Penguin (1978).
Watzlawick, P., Weakland, Ch.E. and Fisch, R. *Principles of Problem Formation and Problem Resolution.* Norton (1974).

ON SOCIETY, MYTHOLOGY AND CULTURE
Eliot, A. *The Timeless Myths: How Ancient Legends Influence the Modern World.* Truman Talley (1997).
Gay, P. *The Cultivation of Hatred.* Fontana (1995).
Harris, M. *Cows, Pigs, Wars and Witches: The Riddles of Culture.* Fontana (1977).
Barthes, R. *Mythologies.* Translated from the French by Annette Lavers. Paladin (1973).
Dunning, A.J. *Extremes: Reflections on Human Behaviour.* Translated from the Dutch by Johan Theron. Harcourt Brace Jovanovich (1992).
Mennell, S. *Norbert Elias: An Introduction.* Blackwell (1992).
Rank, O. *The Myth of the Birth of the Hero* (ed. Philip Freund). Vintage (1932).
Zeldin, T. *An Intimate History of Humanity.* Minerva (1995).

ON GROUP DYNAMICS, PSYCHOLOGY AND PSYCHOTHERAPY
Brown, D. and Zinkin, L. (eds.) *The Psyche and the Social World: Developments in Group-Analytic Theory.* Routledge (1994).
De Maré, P.B. *Perspectives in Group Psychotherapy: A Theoretical Background.* George Allen and Unwin (1972).
Foulkes, S.H. and Anthony, E.J. *Group Psychotherapy: The Psychoanalytic Approach.* Karnac (1965).
Gay, P. *Freud for Historians.* Oxford University Press (1985).
Ormay, A.P. Tom *The Social Nature of Persons: One Person is No Person.* Karnac (2012).
Pertegato, E.G. and G.O. Pertegato (eds). *From Psychoanalysis to Group Analysis: The Pioneering Work of Trigant Burrow.* Karnac (2013).
Pines, M. *Circular Reflections: Selected Papers on Group Analysis and Psychoanalysis.* Jessica Kingsley (1998).
Schermer, V. and Pines, M. (eds.) *Ring of Fire: Primitive Affects and Object Relations in Group Psychotherapy.* Routledge (1994).
Stacey, R. *Complexity and Group Processes: A Radically Social Understanding of Individuals.* Routledge (2003).

Index